OVER-THINKING IN YOUR UNDERWEAR

HARNESS YOUR OVERTHINKING BRAIN FOR SELF-DISCOVERY INSTEAD OF TOTAL SABOTAGE

"Realizations are the worst."
—Tina Fey as Liz Lemon, *30 Rock*

A NOTE BEFORE WE BEGIN:

Names have been changed, details augmented, places revised. What I'm saying is, some stories include fabrications or what Tina Fey calls "joke lies" in her book *Bossy Pants*. I'm not actually worried you'll be confused or thrown by these minor fibs. I just want to mention Tina Fey twice before chapter one, so you'll subconsciously find this book more amusing. Let me know how that works out.

FORETHOUGHT

When you type "overthinking" into a search engine, results populate that sound something like this: "How can I stop overthinking? Is overthinking considered a mental disorder? Will overthinking kill me?"

Okay, calm down, internet!

Since you're standing in a bookstore (Do those still exist?), thumbing a title on the subject, I'll assume, like me, you have an eye for a little analysis. If overthinking were a sport, you would've been signed right out of high school. Your love life, your kids, and your career are overworked in that big, beautiful brain of yours to the point you can't remember why you started ruminating in the first place.

As we plunge into this overthinking pool together, we can agree there's a line where the everyday evaluation gets to be too much and you find yourself lying on the kitchen floor wondering who decided breakfast foods were suited for morning and who chose dinner grub as a thing we do after five. Were there committees? Was voting involved? Did anyone lobby for breakfast nachos, and if they did, how hard did they try? I digress.

Here's the saucy secret—front, center, and before we even get our pants off. **If used correctly, our overthinking brains are tools, not torture.** We're going to strap on our overthinking caps with the intention of eventually taking them off and living happier and more present lives. Whether it's our self-worth, our relationships, or our failures, let's overthink it, learn from it, and leave it in the past where it belongs. We're going to "pick it up and put it down." The "picking it up" part, we're nailing, right? It's putting it down that makes us lighter, easier, and more available for the good stuff coming our way.

Underqualified overthinker

If you're looking for a literary tome with phrases like "double-blind study," written by a Harvard PhD, this is not the book for you. If you're looking for a book by a girl who went to school in the middle of Missouri—who could hardly pass freshman algebra or a breathalyzer test for four and half years—I'M. YOUR. GAL. A girl who's tried, failed, tried again, and finally figured it out over the age of forty with a mason jar of life lessons and enough self-help books under her bed to make it teeter a bit to the left, yep that's me.

Through all the books, podcasts, articles, workshops, meditations, energy healers, mediums, hypnotists, and yes ... years and years of therapy, here's what I can tell you:

If you're on a quest to "be a better you," "live your best life," or "dance like the internet is watching," it begins with some overthinking in your underwear. But after all the navel-gazing, we should be looking up and outward instead of staring at the lint pooling in our belly button. That's the goal for my life, and it's my goal for *you*.

Overthinking meets oversharing

This isn't *just another manic memoir*, so you won't see a chronological look at my life throughout the chapters. You'll find a story here and an anecdote there, which I hope gives you a sense of who I am. I don't have a zillion followers on Instagram, and I'm not trying to secure a podcast for my dog. I'd venture to guess you and I are pretty similar. I'm someone who's taken a lot of swings and seen her share of misses. A girl who's always searching and constantly learning. I'm a lifelong writer who's done everything from advertising copy to greeting cards to failed books and screenplays but whose biggest side hustle is my own personal growth.

But, this book isn't about me,* it's about you. My stories are here to help overthink your life and share concepts in a way that's relatable outside of textbook jargon or complicated spiritual wackery. I hope it's humorous and helpful to you at the same time—sort of like, "ha, ha, hmmm … "

The OG overthinker

Some famous dead guy once said, "a life unexamined is not worth living." Obviously, I know it was Socrates, I have Wikipedia. But, Socrates would FREAKING LOVE ME. My life, my childhood, and my emotions are examined as if they were a crime scene, and I'm on the case taking everything very seriously like that sexy, smart Mariska Hargetheyyyy. That's not how you spell her name, but it's how I shout it at my TV when she walks across the screen. (Try it, it's fun.) Like Mariska, I'm always about to catch the perp who made a mess of my life. Clue: It was me.

No one spends this much time, attention, and co-pays if they're whistling down the road of life. (I don't even know how to whistle.) From an eating disorder to chronic headaches to dating disasters, I've spent my fair share on the detours and delusions that pull us from our purpose.

Because of this, I began overthinking my life years ago. Where do my feelings come from, can I change them, and how can I be the person I envision in my mind? Some things didn't work, but a lot did, and I want to share them with you here.

---

* Okay, it's a little bit about me.

Maybe you're rocking the bottom of a rough phase. We'll get through it, friends. Maybe you want to Stella your groove back after a breakup, divorce, or career setback— we're on it. Or, maybe you're on a continual crusade to win this self-love game. Because, if you aren't singing your praises on the inside, a choir isn't going to burst into song as you walk by.

If I haven't made it clear already, I'm not any sort of thinky scientist person. Coming to me for medical advice would be like going to a tattoo shop for dental work. *"They have the same chairs, how different can it be!?"* Um… different. Fancy degrees or not, I know this much. **You can change your thinking.** Over the years, many books shared concepts, altered my viewpoints, and pointed me in a direction to come whistling out on the other side. I hope this is the beginning, middle, or awe-inspired end of that journey for you.

Our work is separated into four sections. I recommend going in order, but if you feel the need to read backward, standing on your head, or while in the shower, have at it—though some ideas build upon one another, and this book isn't waterproof.

Thinking caps on. Pants off. Let's overthink it.

Part I: Thinking through the fundamentals

We'll strip down to the basics and overthink concepts such as self-worth, our negative labels, core beliefs, inner child, and how that voice in our head informs our self-image. What's up with the Universe anyway? And how can we use it as a guiding force along with meditation and manifestation to unlock a new world for our overthinking brains.

Part II: Thinking through the tough stuff

We'll overthink body image, self-doubt, drinking, failure, and shame. If that doesn't sound like fun, we clearly don't go to the same parties.

Part III: Thinking through relationship business

We'll overthink how we choose our partners and why. We'll get into the seductive subject of Attachment Theory, type, dating, sex, patterns, and how to handle the impact of the ending.

Part IV: Thinking through the voo doo that you do (aka your personal power). We'll take everything we've learned and drive toward our purpose, craft our reality, reframe our perspectives, and use energy to ignite the life we want to live.

On second thought

If you don't get some of my references, you may be … how do I say this? Young. If you find yourself slapping your knee in amusement you may be … not young. Because as I discovered during a failed attempt at TikTok, I'm not young anymore, so my references are from twenty years ago and, come on, no one under thirty slaps their knee.

PART I
THINKING
THROUGH
THE
FUNDAMENTALS

1 CHAPTER
OVERTHINKING SELF-WORTH
not your heroine

I've never done heroin, but one night in 2010 I told a
ballroom of strangers that I loved the junk.

I'm around thirty and recently moved from Missouri
to New York for a job as a copywriter at an ad agency. "Oh,
I bet it's just like *Sex and the City*," everyone says. Despite
being a writer with curly, blonde hair, my weak ankles could
never manage a Manolo and one sip of a cosmopolitan has
me complaining of a sugar headache. I'm what I like to call,
"sitting on the couch" fun.

Now, this is before I harnessed the glory of saying
exactly what you mean. The gorgeous, lusty, power of the
"hard no." Which is how I find myself weak-ankled and
wrangled into one of those charity dating auctions. The kind
where grown men and women stroll onto a stage and drunk
people holler out bids to take them on a date. It's a scene
Carrie Bradshaw might stumble into, but I am not interested
in this episode.

So, here I am trying to squirm out of a situation that
could've been avoided with one, sexy, stand-in-your-worth
word. But "no," I didn't say it.

Leading up to the event, I field a barrage of emails
from an eager, young coordinator, Mallory. Instead of
attacking my apprehension, I fire an arsenal of excuses
Mallory's direction.

"Oops, I have plans that night," I text.

To which she responds, "It's for the orphans."

I lie again with an email, "Mallory, this is awkward, but I'm seeing someone."

"It's not a real date," she counters.

My final attempt is a text claiming, "I get nervous in front of people (scared face emoji)."

Without a pause or a winky-face, Mallory shoots back, "It's not that big of a deal, Lindsay."

The last one is a lie from both parties. I don't get that nervous in front of people, and it's a HUGE deal.

The night of the auction, I arrive to a ballroom in midtown Manhattan. The room tugs at the corners from the pulse of people and sound. I press through a mob of cologne and sweat, estimating the fine for pulling a fire alarm in a crowded venue. I inch my way backstage and reach the lineup of women yanking up their hair and throwing back shots.

One of the women catches sight of me, spins around, and points to my dress, "What kind of flower is that?" she says.

"Hibiscus," I answer without knowing.

"I'm Stacey," she says, bouncing on her toes like a kid waiting for the restroom, "This is my favorite night of the year."

"Really?" I judge.

Looking at Stacey, it registers I missed a dress code memo. Most of the other women are wearing clubwear, of the sequin midriff variety, while I chose a polyester red dress with a flower applique on the shoulder. My outfit analysis is interrupted when Gwen Stefani screams something about "bananas" as the MC for the night takes the stage.

"Who's drunk and ready to save some orphans?" he yells to the crowd. The MC is a fratish 20-something named

Tyson or Bryson or Lysol[*]. He Seacrests around the stage and makes a few obligatory announcements before getting down to business. "And our first bachelorette is Stacey," Tyson says. Stacey hugs me unnecessarily as she bounces toward Tyson, waving her hands in the air *literally* like she just doesn't care.

Tyson continues as a Missy Elliott song blares in the background. "Stacey loves to party. She can't live without Reese's Pieces, and if she were stranded on a desert island, the one thing she'd take with her ... a selfie stick." Stacey[**] works it to the crowd, flips it, reverses it, and dances off stage with a $3,000 bid under her midriff.

The cadence of Tyson's questions shudders me into a pale panic as I think back to a carelessly answered email from three weeks ago. Mallory sent a questionnaire during a busy workday asking me to "quickly fill in a few fun questions and submit my *walk-on music* for the night." With zero context for how it would be used, and a hundred percent confidence I wouldn't be here right now, I answer Mallory's questions like a lazy smartass with no regard for my future self. Recalling this now as I watch the next bachelorette twerk near Tyson, I consider faking a medical emergency but fear my flailing will be interpreted as a dance move.

I lock eyes with Mallory as Tyson says, "And our next bachelorette up for grabs is Lindsay." *Oh my god, this is happening.* My vision tunnels through the spotlight, but a legendary chord progression booms loud and clear.

Dun, Dun, Dun, Dun ... Dun, Dun, Dun, Dun, Dun, DUNNNN ...!

I step onto the stage as "Don't Stop Believin'" thunders in the background. I look out at a sea of blank, boozed-up faces, waiting for me to pout, pose, or drop

---

[*] That can't be right.

[**] I want to pause and say I've dropped more things like they were hot than I can count while wearing body glitter and white eye shadow. I'VE BEEN A STACEY. I've been a Lindsay. I've even been a Lindsay Lohan. I've been all of us through the years. And I'm sure you have too.

something like it's hot. My song selection hits all the wrong notes for this crowd more inclined to "songs about thongs."

But that was only the beginning. Remember the questionnaire? I imagined it printed in a program, and on paper ... my responses seemed amusing, succinctly placed in repetition. If I'm being honest, I wasn't imagining anything. I hoped all of my excuses would exit me out of the situation unfolding before me.

I hear my words escape Tyson's mouth, and I question my answers and my life altogether.

"Lindsay likes heroin," Tyson says. "She can't live without heroin. And if she was stranded on a desert island, the one thing she'd take with her ... heroin." Tyson condemns me with a glance.

The crowd talks, stirs, and clinks glasses. They don't laugh. They don't gasp. They just don't get it. And honestly, I don't either.

"Do I hear fifty dollars?" Tyson asks the crowd.

I walk to the edge of the stage, ignoring that Tyson began the bidding lower than the cost of my subway pass. I smile and wave and possibly curtsey. I point to imaginary friends in the crowd and gesture as if I'm a politician on the campaign trail.

A hand shoots up from a young man in the front row.

"Fifty dollars," he says.

"Do I hear a hundred?" Tyson says with more question in his voice than I appreciate.

"One-hundred," booms a faceless voice from the back.

"Really? Okay," Tyson says. "Do I hear two-hundred?" he continues.

"Two-hundred," slurs a Polo-shirt near the exit.

"Wow, interesting," Tyson says.

A bearded guy by the bar waves his hand and shouts, "Three-hundred."

"Do I hear four-hundred?" Tyson asks.

The room stands still and after another moment, Tyson declares, "Sold, for three-hundred dollars. Have fun with this one."

I shoot Tyson a parting look, solidifying our unsaid feelings for one another and leave with a respectable bid and my self-respect intact.

The night of my assigned date, I show up to the restaurant and see the bearded-bidder sitting at the bar. He seems to have started happy hour yesterday, but I don't mind. It's not a "real date" as Mallory informed me, and I plan to let vodka tonic do the talking for me as well.

After the normal cheers, chit chat, and awkward pauses, I ask my date why he bid on a girl with a taste for heroin and arena rock bands. He pauses a moment and says, "I didn't understand it, but you owned what you were doing, and I liked that."

And THAT is how I met my husband, Joshua.

I'm kidding. I never saw him again, and I certainly don't remember his name.

Confidence is queen

So, was Josh right? Did I understand what I was doing? Am I the heroine of my heroin story? No, absolutely not. It was a colossal mistake like so many mistakes I've made, and I'm sure you have, too. But confidence is standing on stage and waving at a drunk crowd as you hear the ridiculous answers you wrote three weeks ago. It's owning who you are even as you realize you need to exam your sense of humor. It's knowing that Journey is an epic band and that was a super solid song choice, so no regrets there.

Confidence can be faked and faked again. It can be put on and taken off like a polyester red dress with a flower applique on the shoulder. Confidence you throw on for other people, parties, and date auctions. And you snap it off the second you get home like a pinchy bra that's fraying around the edges. You know your confidence is cranking when you see others react to you in a positive manner.

Confidence is the camouflage we wear to hide our true selves in plain sight. It's the "fake it 'til you make it," and the "dress for the part you want" of self-help. It's a necessary accessory as we face the world each day. But, we need to "do the work," dig deep, and make changes from the inside to ensure it isn't all just for show.

Self-worth is the whole kingdom

"The work" begins with our self-worth. It's the single most significant concept to check out in the self-help aisle. **If you cultivate your self-worth and use it as a gauge in every situation, your life and your thinking will change. It's why it's chapter one, it gets top billing and headliner status. Your self-worth is Beyoncé at Coachella.** It deserves attention, adoration, and the same respect we'd give the Queen Bey. You should fawn over it, spoil it, and fall Crazy in Love with every aspect of YOU.

Self-worth and self-confidence reside in the same family, but they're not twins. Confidence is the flashy cousin who wears a lot of makeup and talks too loud at Thanksgiving. Self-worth is the quiet one. You need to pull up a chair and put in the face time to appreciate its meaning in your life. Confidence visits when you put on your favorite sweatpants and your bangs do that one swoopy thing to the side. Self-worth comes from understanding your past, your emotions, and respecting yourself enough to demand everything you desire. No halfsies on your dreams, no settling for the partner who treats you as a room temperature side dish. We are the full eight-course meal at restaurant week, friends.

It's an inside job

There's a fallacy that floats around convincing us that validation comes from partners, peer groups, or the Pulitzer Prize. Self-worth isn't monetized by your salary or quantified by likes on Instagram. It's something you possess as a human being on this planet. You don't have to win an Oscar to earn it or be voted *Sexiest Accountant Alive* to be worthy. It's as easy as saying, "I deserve self-worth." It won't arrive from losing ten more pounds or making $300K a year.

We'll reinforce this idea many times, but it starts right here in the interior of our self-worth. **If we're looking for others to blame or a shaman to heal us, we're taking a trip when the answers are close to home. Everything we do and talk about and overthink—it's an inside job.** Epic levels of self-worth are inside you right now. It's your job to know it, nurture it, and invite it to champion every decision from career choices to who you're meeting for dinner.

I'll have what she's having

I was staring down my fortieth birthday before I learned self-love will save you. Forty years of toying with low self-worth and questioning my value in every conversation. I could fake it like Meg Ryan in that diner scene with Billy Crystal. But self-worth, the golden goose of fulfillment—never met her. *(Mariah Carey voice).* I'd play small, cast away compliments, and let others treat me less than I deserved. Self-worth? She won't stand for it. She'll swoop in, fill you with the light of self-love, and ask (politely, of course) that you make decisions to match your worth.

If you were born before 1980, the modern concept of "self-love" wasn't a word batted around like a baseball in October. In the '60s, activists, community organizers, and "hippies" leaned into self-love and spoke about enlightenment. But as a culture, we're only employing empowerment in the last decade. This leaves generations ready to recalibrate our thinking after a lifetime of missing the mark.

So, where do we start after years of swiping left on ourselves?

The foundation of your self-worth resides in your inner monologue. You may hear the "inner monologue" referred to as "the inner voice," or "the tapes in your head." Whatever you call the "chitty chitty bang bang in your brain" is cool, but understanding its effect on your life is crucial.

Your inner monologue is the supercharged megaphone blaring in your ear since the day you were born. Most of us don't notice our little megaphone except when we're arguing with it about eating an entire sheet cake or texting the date we had last week when we know we shouldn't. But it's always there, even in the small moments. When you become militant about the words, phrases, compliments, and insults flying through your megaphone, you can shape your inner monologue and take command of your self-worth.

Sway your day

Your inner monologue modulates your mood, turning up and down positive and negative emotions based on your thoughts. If you're obsessing over an annoying neighbor, you set the tone, signaling irritation, frustration, and negativity. In your mind, you're throwing mental daggers, when in reality, you're slicing away at your well-being.

You inner monologue creates the atmosphere of your day through positive or negative chatter.

Listen to your monologue and you'll begin to understand your self-worth and your temperament. Be vigilant about the words and phrases wandering through your inner voice. Edit and omit chatter that doesn't yield the emotions or the atmosphere you want to create. Find a phrase to sub-in every time you take a tangent. Maybe it's "I'm grateful for my family." Choose something that feels true and real for you. Like any habit, redirecting your monologue takes time. But eventually, you won't have to overthink it, and your souped-up speech will be a powerful tool on your overthinking journey.

Tank your self-worth

Imagine this ... you have a tank of self-worth inside you. Yes, that's right, an actual vessel at the center of your stuffing. Decorate it with glitter and write your name on the side. Interpret your "self-worth tank" anyway you'd like, but it's filled with hot, bubbly self-worth generated by YOU. See it, meditate on it, and hoard your self-worth as if it were toilet paper in 2020. Here's the takeaway of this rather ridiculous exercise. You control your self-worth tank on a daily, even hourly basis, filling it and using it to guide situations, relationships, and decisions in your life.

For instance, when you're in a dating or relationship situation, get honest with yourself before the appetizer arrives. Do you have to continually compromise yourself to be with this person or make excuses for their behavior? After every date, is your self-worth tank full? Or, is this person draining you through slights and disrespect?

Ask this simple question: *"Does this person fill my self-worth tank or drain it?"*

You're fighting for your self-worth. If someone is punching back and pulling from your progress, why would you allow them in your life?

The same evaluation can be done with friends, family, career, and behaviors. *"Does this person, job, glass of tequila fill my self-worth tank or drain it?"* When you audit your life through the almighty epicenter of self-worth, you demand more from yourself, others, and the Universe.

In the "no"

So, flashback to 2010. Sure, my camouflage of confidence kept me from melting into a flowered-dress puddle that night. But, if I had been acting from a space of self-worth, I wouldn't have been there in the first place. I would've breezily said, *"No,* I'm not much of a bachelorette auction person" instead of people-pleasing my way into a situation that wasn't pleasing to me. Self-worth means owning your "no" and empowering your "yes" in a way that you don't overthink decisions on the other side. It means placing the highest bid on your self-worth and putting it center stage for every moment of your life.

Let's overthink it

Cultivating self-worth takes time, repetition, and a daily commitment to yourself. But the exercises are straightforward and easy to do.

To get started, grab a notebook, a writing utensil, and open to a blank sheet of paper. Find a quiet spot to sit where you can overthink your thoughts. Now, write every positive thing about yourself. Even, "Babies laugh at my funny faces." That's a thing. Write it now, you're a "baby clown."

Here's how a self-love list might look:
Funny
Sensitive
Kind
Good with numbers
Dogs love me
Good at my job
Smart
Punctual
Breakfast sandwich artist

Now that you have this inventory of attributes, keep it nearby, because if you're like me, you'll need it to replace the negative nonsense you've been shouting for years. In the following chapters, we'll listen to that chatter, so we can turn down the noise in our overthinking brains.

2 CHAPTER
OVERTHINKING LABELS
mild child

I'm the kid who did exactly as my parents instructed. I'm what you would call a rule follower, a straight arrow, or what my sister, Kerri, called, "boring." Kerri was "the wild one." Because of this juxtaposition, I've always sustained we are reactions to our siblings. There's a calm one and hyper one. A studious one and an artsy one. A loud one and a quiet one. My research on sibling theory is based on the eight to ten families I observed growing up, so don't look for my white paper anytime soon.

"She was really boring."—my sister, Kerri

If a group of us spent the night at a friend's house whose parents were a bit lax with the curfews and plans were made to sneak out, I stayed back to keep the family dog company. I didn't want to get in trouble. Didn't like to lie. Couldn't handle the guilt associated with a middle school sneak out, so I decided I was better off cuddling with Connie.* This made the facts of one summer night in 1994 all the more perplexing for my mother.

I don't know if this is exclusive to my middle-of-the-map, or if it rings true to your upbringing, but there was an activity in our high school that involved drinking cheap wine coolers in a church parking lot. There wasn't a name

---

* "Connie" was the name of the dog. Try to keep up, please.

for it, but if you pressed me, I'd call it *Holy Hangover* or *Passion of the Smirnoff Ice* if I was feeling theatrical.

This wasn't totally my scene. Sure, I'd go to the parking lot to be with my friends, but I didn't do much drinking in those days, as to avoid previously stated "trouble and guilt." One night, something came over me, and I end up in the back of Sacredwoods Baptist with a few friends, including Bartles and Jaymes.

After a few drinks, the neighborhood cops pull up to end our little party. The red and blue lights flash before my eyes along with my life as "the good kid." My friends are taken to the station, but because of my age, an officer drops me at my house (all of two blocks away).

My mother answers the door in her nightgown and strains to piece together the situation in real-time.

"Ma'am, we have your daughter in the squad car. We found her drinking in the church parking lot up the way," the officer says.

"Kerri." My mom states without question in her voice.

My sister watches the scene unravel from upstairs and defends herself from the second floor, "Mom! I'm home. I've been home for a week, I'm grounded!"

Genuine confusion follows as the officer retrieves me from the car and walks me inside.

My mother can't fathom how I, the good one, could act outside her perception of me so she asks, "Did Kerri have anything to do with this?"

I puzzle my brain for a way to pin this on my older sister but decide it's my cross to bear, "Not really," I say, splitting the difference.

My mother thanks the officer and tells me we'll discuss things in the morning.

I spend the night tossing and turning. Partly from the cheap watermelon syrup mixing with the gas station taquito I had for dinner, but mostly from the fear of my fate. Extra chores? Infinite grounding? No Nintendo? It was worse. The next day, my parents and I have one of those "we're not mad at you, we're just disappointed" discussions. Punishment is one thing, but "disappointment" is psychological warfare, parental style. The admonishment struck me straight in the marrow of my "good kid" label, and they knew it.

Heavy halo

Being "the good kid" has its benefits and its drawbacks. You may avoid the brunt of the blame when it comes to childhood antics, but lug around a perfectionist complex that has you showing up to meetings fifteen minutes early and apologizing to the leg of a chair for your clumsiness.

I'm sure you have a label that's easy to peel away. Maybe you were anointed the musician of the family, the athlete, or the one who would do something ahhh-mazing. We all have labels we may not observe in ordinary life but they influence us in good and bad ways, affecting our behavior and perceptions of ourselves. As easily as we gather good labels, we also pick up a truckload of negative notions. These are the labels we need to overthink, understand, and strike from our inner monologues.

Shadow boxer

Our negative labels begin to shine a light on what Swiss Mister psychologist, Carl Jung, called "the shadow self." The shadow is formed during childhood and follows us the rest of our life if we don't sit down, stare at it across the breakfast table, and have a reckoning.

For our purposes, we're going to simplify aspects of Jung's theory in terms of "labels." Shadow work is a complex subject with layers that take an entire book to digest. If the concept of "labels" appeals to you, see the back of this book for resources on shadow work.

The stuff that sticks

It's not hard to hear our negative labels. They're yammering over our inner monologue like the most annoying guest at a party. *Pipe down, Tiffany!* They're locked and loaded with insecurities and ready to remind us when things go wrong or get a bit quiet. Negative labels are words such as "ugly, fat, stupid, failure, incompetent, weak, or sick." *I know, fun, right?*

The call is coming from inside the house

As I began to monitor my inner monologue, I was knocked over by negativity. Phrases buzzed from ear-to-ear such as, "I'm not smart enough for that job." Or, "He'd never go out with me." Or even, "I'm such a bad driver." And, here's the thing, *I am such a bad driver.* I once ran under a school bus because I didn't look both ways before pulling into an intersection. *Yellow, black stripes, the size of a small strip mall—that kind of school bus.* But even this bulls-eye accurate self-slight is one I don't need to replay every time I get behind the wheel. A- It's makes me nervous as I drive. B- It doesn't add to my overall self-worth, and that's the noise we are shutting up, turning off, closing down for business.

Note: No school children were hurt in the writing of this paragraph. The bus was empty but for a very nice driver.

Your inner monologue streams a 24-hour news cycle straight to your brain. If "I'm the emperor of all idiots" runs on repeat, it doesn't matter if it's fake news. **We believe the words we tell ourselves and every utterance informs our self-worth.**

Crating a positive inner monologue is paramount to the rest of the work we do in this book. Choose your words with care and harness a hype squad that's cheering so loud your teeth are chattering.

Check your reflection in your projections

When I wrote greeting cards, I had a line that said, "May you find someone who ignores you long enough that you like them." I gave it to many, many friends. I should've also licked a stamp, plopped it in the mail, and sent it special delivery to myself. Here's the deal, WE'RE ALWAYS TALKING TO OURSELVES. When you offer advice, pass judgment, or write a greeting card, you're saying loud and proud what gets-you-in-the-gut about your own behavior.

If you missed PSYCH 101 and every reality show over the past fifteen years, this is what we call "Projecting." Projecting goes something like this: "I have a terrible anger management problem, so I'll point my finger or flip a table and say, "NO, YOU HAVE ANGER ISSUES, PAMELA!" We deflect our undesirable characteristics onto people around us, calling them out to others, or ourselves, rather than dealing with our own issues.

To overplay this reality metaphor, projections are the Kardashians of psychology. Everyone knows about them, everyone talks about them, and everyone pretends they're not totally into them ... but they are.

Our labels live in our reactions to situations and people. If you have trouble finding your negative labels, check your reflection in your projections.

Some time ago, I found some less-than-lovely labels lurking in my projections. I was collaborating with a small team on a branding project. Things were going along as expected until one of my coworkers missed deadlines, didn't follow through, and sporadically turned in their part of the work. Zero on the teammate scale, right? But, here's the thing ... their behavior didn't affect my ability to do my job, get a paycheck, or yell at the TV as I watch Bravo. They didn't infringe on my life AT ALL, yet they were scratching me like sand in my bikini on a 100-degree day. Who acts so irresponsible? Were they completely incompetent? How unreliable can one person be? Itch. Itch. Itch.

Overthink events or people if they A- can't be avoided* B- keep reappearing in different forms C- bother you in disproportion to their weight.

While I was frustrated, I was also confused why I cared so much. To no surprise, I found "irresponsible,

---

* It's your mother-in-law.

incompetent, and unreliable" are words that live in my
negative labels. What I projected onto this coworker came
from my past. It took a bit of overthinking because I don't
see myself that way now. But when I started my career, I
did. These were labels I feared the most. In fact, as I was
learning my way, you can bet I *was* all of those things. So
over the years, I worked hard to be the definitional
opposite. And now, when I see these traits peek out in
another person—I go judge-and-jury in a hurry. As with
most things in life, the ruling wasn't about them, it was
about me. What gets us heated about others, is an indicator
of what's burning up inside us. Instead of going on a trip
about someone else, use that spark as a wayfinder toward
your labels.

Be a label maker

If we look at our labels, positive or negative, where
did they come from? And more importantly, are they ours?
Who gave you this label and do you want it? Don't accept a
label you didn't earn. Even if you salted the rim on that label
of "world's worst drinker of margaritas"—you don't have to
carry it around. *Pick it up and put it down.* See why it's there
and decide it's no longer yours to own.

My list of labels doesn't start and stop with "the
good kid." When I take the time to sit with my list, I'll get
to "sick, weak, and small." I had a lot of headaches growing
up and an eating disorder throughout middle school and
high school. Because of this, my family often treated me as
a fragile being about to break. Even as an adult with a ham
sandwich in my hand, I felt there was something wrong
with me, regardless of what had come together in my life.
This was only my perception, but that's the thing about
labels, they're sticky. It's hard to wipe them clean until you
see they're a sigh from the past and not a full-throated
reflection of who you are now.

Let's overthink it

To get started, grab a notebook, a writing utensil, and open to a blank sheet of paper. Find a quiet spot to sit where you can overthink your thoughts. Let's monitor your monologue for a day or two, noting labels as they arise. On the left side of your paper, list the positive labels you hear. On the right side, list the negative labels that come up for you. Notice, did you observe, "Wow, I'm an unbelievable mother" as you helped your child with homework. Or, did you say, "I'm such a nitwit" when you couldn't log into your fourteenth Zoom call of the week? Listen to your labels and take them seriously. Labels such as "nitwit" may seem small, but they add up over time, scratching away at your self-worth.

Flip the script

- Look at the list of labels you gathered. If your positive side is long and strong, congratulations, you can stop reading this book. (JOKES!)
- Look at your negative labels. From now on, and I mean EVERY SINGLE TIME you hear a negative label stop ... and replace it with a word or phrase from your "self-love" list at the end of chapter one. For instance, you catch yourself saying, "I'm the master of all mess-ups." Nope, no, zip it. Now repeat, "I am smart and capable. I am smart and capable."

3 CHAPTER
OVERTHINKING CORE BELIEFS
the solitary truth

My parents make friends on vacation. They attend high school reunions. A run to the store with my mother my take upwards of two-hours as she chats with a woman in produce about the fall weather or a fall she took last year.

In juxtaposition, I've taken international vacations alone and spoke solely to the person at hotel check-in with a slight nod. The only reunions I attend involve Bravo Andy. If I'm speaking with someone at the grocery store, call 9-1-1 because I'm informing them of a medical emergency.

Growing up with the most extra of 'verted parents, I believed this was normal human behavior. Plan parties, join the club, know your neighbors. Let me be clear, my parents are two of my favorite people to be around. But as an introvert who covets quiet, needs periods of recharge, and likes my social time in small doses, I thought my mom and dad got a defective product they should return to Amazon.

I absorbed the core belief "extroversion is normal," and introversion? Well, it wasn't an idea we talked about in the '80s or posted as a badge of honor on our non-existent social media sites. Even now, I typed, "introvert" into an online thesaurus and the words "shy," "nerd," and "misfit," popped up along with many more unflattering labels. *Thanks again, internet!* But these labels, among others, are how I felt for a long time because who I am didn't line up with the core belief I saw at home.

Core beliefs are the absolute truths we hold about the world and how it functions.

We adopt core beliefs from our parents, caretakers, siblings, friend groups, and our community. Adopting a belief system that works against you can influence how you feel about yourself and your self-worth. Those negative labels from chapter two are grounded in our past and formed from concepts such as core beliefs. Core beliefs may look and sound something like:

- The world is a scary place. Or (I am safe in the world.)
- I am unlovable. Or (I am lovable.)
- I am a failure. Or (I will be successful.)
- I am stupid. Or (I am smart.)
- I am unlucky. Or (I am one of the lucky ones.)
- I am untalented. Or (I am talented.)
- I am ugly. Or (I am beautiful.)
- Life is unfair. Or (If you act accordingly, the word is a fair place.)
- Being a single mom is bad. Or (Single moms are strong and inspiring.)
- It's impossible to get ahead. Or (If you work hard, you will make it.)
- All marriages end in divorce. Or (Marriage is forever.)
- Men (or women) always cheat. Or (Relationships are filled with safety and commitment.)
- Being an introvert is weird. Or (Introversion is normal.)

Core beliefs don't only thrive on a positive/negative axis. They also hang in the balance which takes a bit of overthinking. Imagine you grew up with the belief, "Everyone gets married by thirty." It's a sentiment you observed in your community and it took shape as a core belief. Now, you're twenty-eight, packing your bags to travel the world with no interest in partnership and something seems wrong about stamping your passport. You're responding to a core belief and letting it cloud your current perspective. Understand the origin of your belief and hand over its walking papers if it doesn't fit the life you want to live.

Look what you made me do

As you poke through your past, your pointer finger may start working overtime. My parents did THIS and my environment caused THAT. Blame releases us from the responsibility of our emotions and actions.

People, institutions, society, history, it all deserves scrutiny and accountability in many, many cases. But this chapter isn't about grabbing a cape and avenging wrongdoing. It's about mastering your life and not letting an ounce of your personal power slip through the seams.

If every time something goes wrong, we think, "I'm from a broken home" or "I had a bad marriage," you're removing authority over your emotions and current actions and placing the blame squarely in the past. **Recognize the source of your label or core belief and work through it** (with a professional if necessary). But after the analysis, *pick it up and put it down*, so you're in control, not limiting beliefs from long ago.

Today, I wear my introversion like a timeworn pair of sweatpants. I lock the door, cuddle my dog, and decline your invitation like an incoming SPAM call. I know introversion is a normal, healthy personality type as much as its outgoing alter ego, extroversion, and I have no desire to feel sorry about it. Being an introvert made me the writer, overthinker, and wellness-obsessed searcher I am today. It turns out, "introversion" is the only club I'd race to join, and in here, it's always a party of one.

Let's overthink it

To get started, grab a notebook, a writing utensil,

and open to a blank sheet of paper. Find a quiet spot to sit where you can overthink your thoughts. Try to expand the list of core beliefs below based on your upbringing. Core beliefs are personal to your past, and they span wide and winding subjects. Again, core beliefs may look and sound something like this:

- The world is a scary place. Or (I am safe in the world.)
- I am unlovable. Or (I am lovable.)
- I am a failure. Or (I will be successful.)
- I am stupid. Or (I am smart.)
- I am not lucky. Or (I am one of the lucky ones.)
- I am untalented. Or (I am talented.)
- I am ugly. Or (I am beautiful.)
- Life is unfair. Or (If you act accordingly, the word is a fair place.)
- It's impossible to get ahead. Or (If you work hard, you will make it.)
- All marriages end in divorce. Or (Marriage is forever.)
- Men (or women) always cheat. Or (Relationships are filled with safety and commitment.)
- Being a single mom is bad. Or (Single moms are strong and inspiring.)
- Being an introvert is weird. Or (Introversion is normal.

After you're finished, look at your list and/or the examples above and ask yourself, "How does this statement make me feel?" It doesn't take much overthinking to know "I am smart" adds to your life in a healthy way and even propels you forward. However, if you look at "I am a failure," and say it out loud, maybe it stings a little, and resonates as a core belief from your past. Find your core beliefs, understand their origin, and *pick it up and put it down.* Don't carry a core belief that isn't yours and let it stick to you in a way that influences your self-worth and even the decisions you make in your life.

Strengthen your core

Invent a new list of core beliefs to replace any negative notions you noticed. This is your chance to upend your negative labels and completely reshape your inner monologue.

For example, change "I am a failure" to "I am erupting with talent and destined for Broadway." Write it down, and say it over and over. See how it feels running through your head. Do it consistently until it replaces your core belief of "failure." When we get to meditation in chapter five, use a few of those Zen'd out moments to practice your mega-charged inner monologue.

Brief Thoughts

Advice I give myself while staring in the mirror

+ Don't use your "dog voice" around people you just met.

+ A side-ponytail isn't saying what you think it's saying.

+ That spray tan is going to rub off at the most embarrassing time you can imagine.

+ Gluten-free cupcakes aren't a superfood.

+ Don't wave at the end of a Zoom call. You look like a grandma on a cable commercial.

4 CHAPTER
OVERTHINKING YOUR INNER CHILD
no kids' stuff

"I've never really had a headache," is something people have said to me on occasion. They may as well have said, "I never tasted pizza." Or, "Who's this Jennifer Aniston you speak of?"

You see, I've had a headache for more days of my life than I haven't. Headaches are so common for me, I assume they're laced into the fabric of everyone's day like teeth brushing and eating a block of cheese in the bathtub. Some days, they're small, minor, so distant I wouldn't worry it was there unless you mention it. Others, it's acute and enveloping, as if a lightning bolt struck the right side of my head and an electric current throbs for hours, if not days.

Beginning about six-years-old, I start getting immobilizing headaches. They creep over the front of my forehead and wrap around the back of my neck and they happen every day without fail. I can count on nothing more than the pain coming on after morning recess and before lunch. My parents take me to see a neurologist and my CAT scan says all was well as far as my medulla and oblongata are concerned. The headaches continue through my teens, not debilitating, but present like a chaperone making sure you aren't having too much fun.

When I'm about twenty-five, my headaches throw a house party, inviting over nausea, dizziness, flashing lights, and ringing in my ears. They level up to migraines and flatten me in the process. I tell myself the pain isn't real, and it's all in my mind. And that's one of the hardest things about migraines, and headaches in general, they feel like an overworked cliché. "Not tonight, dear, I have a headache." Or, "Don't bother her, she has a migraine." It's something you say about a person who isn't holding it together instead of a chronic condition that comes on without warning and seems to elude a cure by the medical community. No matter the head games, the pain won and it wasn't going anywhere.

I find medicines that work and then stop. Therapies that feel promising, and eventually, not so much. In no specific order, here are the (-ist), medicines, and otherwise, I try for my migraines—a neurologist, a craniosacral specialist, an audiologist, a neurological ophthalmologist, a paleontologist (making sure you're awake), a therapist, an energy healer, a nutritionist, an acupuncturist, a hypnotist, herbs, antidepressants, beta-blockers, triptans, anti-seizure medicines, peptide receptor shots, Botox, and one very weird naturalist in Colorado who tells me I'm probably wearing my hats too tight. If you're picturing me in some sort of chic fedora while speaking to this "doctor," you'd be forgiven. In actuality, I'm not wearing a hat then (or ever) which makes his advice all the less useful.

I sign up for seminars and workshops promising enlightenment on the level of Tony Robbins and private one-on-one sessions with spirit guides attempting to balance my meridians. If there's a chance you have the answer to something, anything ... I'll pay you 20-200 dollars and buy the commemorative crystal afterward.

To no surprise, the label "sick" clings to me like a pair of SPANX at an outdoor wedding. When I think back to my first memory living with this label, it hits around kindergarten or first grade.

This day wasn't like other days. This day ... I'm wearing shorts with a belt. Shorts with a belt are the ceiling of excitement for a first grader, second only to shoes with Velcro. The thick, leather belt entertains during lessons and makes me feel like a tiny executive delivering "The Pledge of Allegiance" to a class full of subordinates. But around lunchtime, I feel a crunching in my brain. Now, I'm home, crying and disappointed my day didn't meet the promise of my wardrobe.

When I think back to that little lady in the belted-shorts, she feels small, fragile, and weak. Label, label, la-la-la-label. She didn't see herself as strong, healthy, or even capable of maneuvering in the world. Understanding ourselves as children helps grasp the origin of many of our emotions and actions as an adult. This is where inner child work enters the chat. "You up?"

Out there

Your inner child is exactly how it sounds. It's the "little you" from the past who needs to heal a wound or rewrite a story to see yourself in a healthier way. It sounds a bit "out there." We've moved from solid concepts like "self-worth" to a commune in the desert where a woman named "Moonbeam" gifts you a basket made of macramé. Hang with me, inner child work is still on solid ground. It's another self-help tool that's easy to follow and ultimately educates and grows our self-worth.

When we look back at the *little you* who struggled with a health issue, grew up in poverty, or generally hated third grade, we begin to comprehend the adult you are now.

Let's assume you were bullied as a child. Now you're a successful frozen yogurt mogul with decades between you and recess ridicule. Yet, every piece of feedback from a consumer or employee invites your inner child to the boardroom. You hit back, become defensive, and feel attacked. Until you work through your past, your inner child shows up to every meeting. In other words, you relive your childhood emotions because you never addressed them years ago. Moving passed the playground requires meeting your inner child, understanding what they need, and letting go of old labels that live rent-free in your head.

Present day adult

Today, my headaches are manageable, absent somedays and engrossing on others. But I don't feel "sick" anymore. The label doesn't run through my head like the ticker tape at the bottom of the CNN screen. I met my inner child and gave her what she needed to let go of a story she learned in grade school. Even though the symptoms aren't totally alleviated, the label is.

Let's overthink it

To get started, grab a notebook, a writing utensil, and open to a blank sheet of paper. Find a quiet spot to sit where you can overthink your thoughts.

Think back to a childhood memory that holds particular weight. These memories may be tied to your labels or core beliefs from chapters one and two. Examples include: learning your parents were getting a divorce, being bullied in school, or the death of a family member or friend.

As you envision this memory, what did the little version of you (your inner child) feel at this moment. Examples include: scared, unsafe, small, sad, or anxious.

Do you see these emotions appearing in your adult life? In other words, where do you see your inner child showing up in the present day? Examples include: Lack of confidence at work, codependence in relationships, general anxiety, etc.

With this knowledge, what does your inner child need? Examples include: safety, consistency, self-confidence.

Awareness is a powerful awakening, but let's take it a step further to help you escape the six year old yelling for attention.

Find a baby picture of yourself (0-3 years old). Using this image as reference, write a letter to this child, expressing what you wish you had known at the time. Ex: "You are safe, you are worthy, you are strong, you are healthy, you will overcome this situation."

Place this image where you will see it every day (near your laptop). On a Post-It note, write a phrase from your "inner child letter" and stick the note to the image. The phrase may be "You are confident and strong." Now, each time you glance at the picture, you have a quick, daily exercise to nurture your inner child.

Finally, when we get to chapter five, use this picture in a visualization through meditation. Sit in meditation and imagine this "little you" safe and happy. Then, watch yourself grow and change through the years, all the way up to the present day, but this time with the ("confidence, strength, safety") you didn't have in real life.

There are countless forms of inner child work and many ways to attach to your past, heal, and move forward. If you're interested in this topic, many of the workshops and books listed in the back go further into this learning.

5 CHAPTER
OVERTHINKING MEDITATION & MANIFESTATION
ohm, shanti, shanti, shit

My path to enlightenment begins at a nine-dollar-a-month gym. I took advantage of one of those introductory offers where a pushy "fitness ambassador" attempts an upgrade to a more expensive package like I'm a senior on a timeshare tour in Boca.

I chose the gym for its proximity to my apartment, which is how I know the poorly painted over smell wafting between air freshener and workout stench is tortilla chips. The space used to house a Mexican restaurant and oil from the deep fryers lingers in memoriam.

As I exit a spin class, a man in a tiny tank top presses into me, leaving his sweat across my body as a DNA-filled calling card. The sticky affront is enough to make me throw in the towel and commit to a life of chair aerobics in my living room, but then I notice it ... a flyer for a "FREE YOGA CLASS AND INNER PEACE." I'm curious about a practice that birthed the arms of Madonna and the soul of Sting. But mostly, I want out of the meat market madness of my current routine.

Welcome to my Ohm

Entering my first yoga class, I'm greeted by hushed whispers, intimate lighting, and pillows strewn delicately on the floor. The space is gently heated, and we're told to "move at your own pace" by a ballerina-figured woman who speaks of her feelings and asks me to consider mine. At the end, we lie on our backs for something she calls "savasana," and I call "a nap." Yoga brings together everything I adore: intense introspection bordering on over analysis and curling into the fetal position in the middle of the day. I'm in—big time.

So for the past fifteen years, I've been going to yoga consistently and talking about it constantly. If you ask friends to describe me in a word, they'll get to "yoga" pretty fast. If granted a few more syllables, they'll get to, "annoying about yoga" even faster. I'm one of *those* people. I say, "chakra alignment," and "third eye center" as if I'm the Dalai Lama in Lululemon.

I've gone on wooded yoga retreats and taken classes atop buildings in the city. I've done spiritual workshops bathed in a sound bath and moved through hip hop flows with a DJ jamming in the corner. But all the while, there's part of my practice I was faking, phoning in, sleeping through.

At the end of every class, the teacher takes you through a guided meditation. Close your eyes, turn off the ratta-tat-tat in your mind, and find a space of peace. For over a decade, I used this time to organize to-do lists in my head or plot my escape from a high-stakes hostage situation. I wasn't so much Zen'd out as I was zoning out on the most essential part of this ancient art.

I finally gave over to meditation out of sheer desperation. After working in advertising my entire career, I quit my safe, 401K-laced, benefit-having job, and took the leap to freelance writing. If ever there was a time to cut the negative chatter and find a few blissed-out moments, it was now.

Meditation

To no surprise, I'm a person who slips "Have you tried meditation?" into conversations with a friend, date, or grocery delivery driver. As it comes out of my mouth, I feel the person look at me a bit different. Maybe not from the guy delivering my groceries, I'm wearing a robe with a T-shirt over it, I already lost him.

Anyway, I'm a "person who talks about her meditation practice," and that's a whole other level of "woo-woo" reserved for ketamine enemas and vaginal eggs. Once you begin meditation, you realize why people feel compelled to hype it up and share it with others, because it feels like a bit of witchcraft. The kind that casts a spell and relieves an underlying hum of anxiety that nags at us all. That little verve of energy that propels you some days and leaves you lying on the floor overthinking in your underwear on others.

As you begin to develop a practice, there are many apps to guide you through the process in an easy, understandable way. You can choose custom options for sleep, stress relief, or even "meditation while walking." There are free versions or upgraded programs that require a small fee.

If you need more guidance, look for a meditation process that assigns an individual teacher for support. These methods usually center around learning a mantra or a word and repeating it as a pathway to clear your mind and elevate your consciousness. They range in price and can be expensive, but the training is personalized, attentive, and lasts a lifetime.

When I first began meditating, I started with a free app and quickly decided I was more comfortable with my own cobbled-together practice. I'll share a bit of my process with you here and throughout the rest of the book.

To get started, find a place to sit quietly without being interrupted. If it's a space that brings you peace, all the better. Sit cross-legged or lie down. Close your eyes and clear your mind. Focus on the feeling of your breathing or the sound of your breath. In the beginning, even a few short minutes is a lot to ask of our overthinking brains. Shoot for five minutes and add time to the clock each day until you reach twenty minutes.

In meditation, repetition is part of the relaxation, quieting your mind, and becoming present. I sit with my eyes closed and visualize myself in a space that brings a sense of calm (sitting on a beach, on a mountain, at the lake). I project warmth wrapping around me. I feel relaxed, and it takes me to a place outside the blackness of closing my eyes and clearing my mind.

For me, here's the real hack. I turn on binaural beats in my headphones. The tones fill the space in my head and allow me to focus on my breathing rather than the chatter in my mind. After twenty minutes, I feel lighter, calmer, and sometimes a problem I was turning over becomes clearer.

Many people recommend the benefits of a twenty-minute practice, twice daily. Much like exercising before work, this is a nice idea that you'll probably snooze through. No doubt, the more meditation the better, but don't twist yourself into a lotus flower trying to cram it into your cranium. Find a few minutes each day and don't stress the specifics.

The Law of Attraction

About fifteen years ago, a style of manifestation called the Law of Attraction was all the rage. From my limited understanding, people could have anything they desire by *thinking it* into existence. A particular example was a woman who spoke about wanting a shiny, red, sports car and "POW," a little red Corvette showed up in her driveway as if she was Prince in the 1980s. That was her *entire* explanation. This manifestation story had more plot holes than my first screenplay. Who drove the car to her house? Was there completed paperwork in the glovebox? Did she check the trunk for a dead body? Because if she didn't, she's not watching enough true crime documentaries to stay alive in the real world.

Despite my confusion, I wanted to believe this is how the Universe works. I sat down, crossed my legs, squinted my eyes closed, held my hands in prayer position, and visualized a check arriving in my mailbox for a million dollars. Why not? If the Universe is out here dropping cars in driveways, surely she can manage an 8x3 piece of paper. As you guessed, nothing happened. Notta thing. I didn't even win the free lunch raffle at my local deli that week. Turns out, I misunderstood the basic concept of the Law of Attraction.

Laying down the law

If your mother ever said, "That attitude isn't going to get you anywhere," she was oh-so-loosely giving you a lesson in the Law of Attraction. Like attracts like. Energy flows where attention goes. The Universe sees our energy and it matches it. It's that simple.

Whatever you're focusing on, you will attract more of into your life. If you're locked into negativity, don't expect greatness. If you're brimming with positive energy and action, good things will follow.

Working with the Law is about raising your energy and vibrations to the level of things, experiences, and opportunities you're calling into your life. And the Law of Attraction is where we meet our manifestations. (More on energy in chapter twenty-two).

Manifestation and intentions

Manifestation begins by getting clear on what you want, setting intentions, believing you deserve it, and putting in the elbow grease to make it happen. It doesn't sound like sorcery when I say it like that, does it? It sounds more like a super, cosmic kick in the pants.

Once you pair manifestation with meditation and a little belief in the Universe—that's where the abracadabra comes in.

Simply put, you set intentions (or goals), take action steps to get there, remove negative behavior (and thoughts), and put faith in the Universe and yourself that you can achieve whatever you set out to do. It's not that it doesn't take work. It just doesn't take a lot of four-syllable jargon to get there.

Write it

To get started, grab a notebook, and a writing utensil. Find a quiet spot to sit where you can overthink your thoughts. Don't imagine your list (though we'll do a bit of that later), but take the care to put it in a notebook you keep in a special place and refer to now and then.

Open to a blank page and write everything you want to call into your life through the manifestation process. This is what we refer to as your "intentions." To me, EVERYTHING is a bit overwhelming. "Slow down, Universe, we just met!" So, I break off bite-sized manifestations. I ask myself, "What do I want this month?" Then, I write it down. I make a new list each month as I put action behind my intentions and make progress with the Universe.

Your list can be lofty, such as "I want a job that pays 250K a year." Or, "about your loft," such as "I want to find the perfect picture for my living room wall." The Universe isn't here to judge. It hears your intention, sees your action, and in time, delivers your manifestations.

In real life, I'm a freelance writer. A few years ago, I was in a slow period. I took out my manifestation list and wrote the intention, "I want to double my earnings every month for the next six months." I decided to put the six-month ticker on it just to see what would happen. It was a stretch to assume the few opportunities trickling in could turn into DOUBLING my best month on a consistent basis. But I wrote it, I meditated on it, and I believed it would happen. A week later, I got a call about a steady writing gig needed over the next few months. I accepted and the following week, I got another call about an equally lucrative job over the same time period, bringing my monthly number to twice what I usually make. I was shocked, and at the same time, I completely felt it was going to happen. I easily hit my number for the next six months which my bank account liked, but the manifester in me LOVED. This was the first time I wrote it, I saw it, and practiced working with the Universe to make it happen.

See it

I watch a lot of sports documentaries. I'm not an athlete, I'm not sporty—I just do it. (Trademark Nike.) As a super fan of this genre, I've seen the mental preparation that goes into winning gold medals and big games. Since the beginning of athletic competition, premiere athletes have used the tool of visualization to center themselves, gain advantage, and concentrate on the moment of winning.

To put it in manifestation terms: 1- They state their intention to the Universe: "to win a gold medal in swimming." 2- They put action behind it and spend hours in the pool and the weight room. 3- They sit in meditation and visualize how it feels to hit the water, pull ahead of the competition, push off the back wall leading the pack, and stand on the podium with a gold medal around their neck. National Anthem playing, crowd cheering, mom crying.

They see every second, and in the end, their swim plays out exactly as it did in their head. Coincidence? No. They prepared their mind for a future reality the same way they prepared their body.

Visualization works in our non-Olympic lives, too. Grab your manifestation list, pair it with meditation, and see your intentions appear in your mind. For instance, close your eyes and visualize your boss walking into your office and saying, "Congratulations, Anna, you got the promotion." Or, imagine your credit card bill arriving. You open it and see a zero balance. Try it for interpersonal situations as well. If you and your partner can't keep it cool every time you discuss how to pay for your kid's college, put a little imagination around it. Visualize the conversation, but this time with the level-headed exchange you desire.

You still have to do the work to impress your boss, pay off that bill, or practice healthy communication (no little red Corvettes are arriving out of nowhere). But believing your manifestations are possible and visualizing it clearly in your mind is an effective tool to get the gold.

Say it

Using affirmations or positive self-talk helps stop negative chatter, elevate our mood, and bring our energy in line with our manifestations. I'm not saying stand in front of the mirror and call yourself a "hot, sexy bitch," though I don't see the harm in that. Meow…

On occasion, I pair words from my self-love list (chapter one) to form affirmations I run through my head during meditation. It may sound something like this: "I am capable. I am confident. I am creative." Afterward, I'm relaxed and closer to the person I'm projecting in my mind. It feels a little Stuart Smalley, but Stuart was good enough, smart enough, and doggone it, so are you.

Behave yourself

None of us like mixed signals. Especially a gal as busy as the almighty Universe. When you set an intention, act accordingly, lining up your behavior with the goal you plan to achieve. If "pay off my debt" is on your list, but you're on a first-name basis with the Amazon guy, your actions aren't lining up with your manifestation. But if you replace online shopping with saving and visiting thrift stores, you signal to the Universe you're ready to receive your manifestation. **Put action steps behind your intentions and watch the Universe deliver your manifestations straight to your door.**

Namaste your way

Meditation isn't mandatory for personal growth. Mindfulness can be anything that resets the racket in your head: Yoga, listening to music, kickboxing, a long run, reading a book, gardening, a walk in the woods, getting your sweat on, lying under the stars, cooking, taking a bath, turning off your phone and social media for twenty-four hours, seeing live music, or watching a stand-up routine. Meditation and finding a moment of peace is personal and up to you. Close your eyes, quiet your mind, chill out your brain, recharge your battery, call a timeout, say namaste, or don't.

Let's overthink it

To get started, grab a notebook, a writing utensil, and open to a blank sheet of paper. Find a quiet spot to sit where you can overthink your thoughts.

Guide to manifesting (a cheat sheet)

- Write it: Decide to write your manifestations once a month or every three months—whatever cadence works for you. Your list can be BIG: I want to start my own cookie company. Or, not so big: I want to eat fewer cookies.
- See it: Through meditation, visualize yourself achieving your manifestations. EX: Visualize your cookie company. Build it in your mind and see yourself standing behind the counter. Pick out the color of the interior and put icing on top of every detail.
- Say it: Add affirmations that line up with your intentions. EX: "I'm the world's best cookie maker." Stir in some words from your self-love list in chapter one to amp up your inner monologue.
- Behave: Make a list of action steps to help you meet your manifestations. EX: Join a small business networking group to learn from others in your community.
- Eliminate the negative: Want to buy a house? Turn off QVC and tune into your frugal side.
- Get your gratitude on: Be thankful for what you have at this very moment. *And*, be grateful for the manifestations you're calling into your life. Don't wait to feel good or feel gratitude. Start now and your manifestations will join you. EX: "I see the future I'm creating, and I'm already thankful for the abundance coming my way."

- Believe you deserve it: You are worthy of the partner who crushes you with compliments or the one-seat-on-the-rocket-to-Mars type opportunity. Expect astronomical things for yourself and the Universe will too.
- Energy-on: Raise your vibrations to the level of experiences you're imagining. (We'll get to energy in chapter twenty-two.)

Overflowing your self-worth (a meditation)

Remember our "self-worth tank" from chapter one? It's that tangible gauge of self-love that resides inside. It's up to us to overflow our self-worth tank or watch it drain without doing a damn thing. Below is a meditation to help you see your self-worth as the incendiary center that guides your life. Use this meditation a few times a week or in the moments you need a shot-in-the-ohm.

Find a quiet meditation space. Sit or lie down, eyes closed. Let yourself ease into the moment for a few minutes focusing on your breath. Imagine a space of calm, peace, and warmth. Now, picture your self-worth as an actual vessel inside you, your self-worth tank. Maybe it sits at the core of your navel or at the center of your heart. See your tank filling with hot, bubbly self-worth. Maybe it's gold or blue or a thick lava-like red. The colorful liquid bubbles up and fills your self-worth tank, sending a rush of warmth throughout your body. Your self-worth continues to rise and explodes from the tank, pouring to your hands and feet in a shock of heat and light. Stay here for a few minutes and enjoy the pulse of this force flowing through you.

Now, imagine you're sitting in a space you find calming (on the top of a mountain, at the lake, in your backyard). Your body is glowing, absolutely radiating with a full tank of self-worth. Stay here for a few minutes. You see the light of your self-worth pan out to the Universe and merge with the manifestations you're calling toward you. Envision a few things from your manifestation list now. Do you see yourself getting the job? Meeting the partner? Whatever is on your list, see it and feel it happening.

Come back to that place of peace and stillness where you started. You are warm, light, and filled by your self-love. Stay this way for as long as you find pleasing. As you leave meditation, you will take this version of yourself out into the world. When you are ready, come out of your meditation and back to your day.

After exercise/self-worth evaluations

As situations arise in your life, from dates to family to career obstacles, use your self-worth as a set point. For instance, the person who never follows through asks you on a date. Or, a co-worker begs you to cover their part of a project AGAIN. Sit in meditation and picture your self-worth tank. Is this situation filling you with self-worth or draining you of self-love? Make decisions and act in a way that honors your self-worth and fills your tank.

6 CHAPTER
OVERTHINKING THE UNIVERSE
what's up?

Growing up my family attends a church that has the spirit of Jesus and the soul of a middle school theater camp. Congregation members share liturgical dances, skits are performed, and spoken word is the norm.

When I bring a boyfriend to a particularly dramatic Easter service, he leans over and whispers, "This is like *Waiting for Guffman*." If you don't get that obscure Christopher Guest reference, know that miming was involved and our family dentist rose from the dead resurrection-style.

In my twenties, I attend a Catholic church with a friend. As we leave the service, I question him in confusion, "You mean to tell me, the same thing happens each week in calm repetition, and *not once* has your mom's friend tap-danced the *Ten Commandments?*" He assures me this is the case. I cross myself and consider becoming Catholic. If nothing else, for the peace, quiet, and super comfy-looking robes.

I assume all churches resemble an intimate community playhouse where every Father's Day you read aloud a haiku while wearing an item of your dad's clothing.

My sister Kerri and I have many inside jokes and stories about the church where we grew up. The pageants where we were a Wise Man or an Oxen—your kids remember dressing as livestock and lying in a field, and they'll make you pay for it (sorry, mom). But I also took away the sense of something bigger. You can't sit through sermons for eighteen years passing notes to your sister without absorbing that "the holy spirit lives in all of us."

How you define that "holy spirit" is up for interpretation and, in my book, it's where all this talk about "the Universe" comes in.

Up until a few years ago, the only person using the phrase "the universe works in mysterious ways" on the reg was Neil DeGrasse Tyson and his friends. Today, every Tom, Dick, and Hari Krishna wag their tongues about the great unknown. So when we reference "the Universe," what are we talking about? Solid. Question.

Rolling in the Prophets

If you're religious, and God is your *guy in the sky* and that's who you pray to when you put your hands together at night or sit in meditation, Amen. I know where you're coming from (*see*: lying in a field /Oxen). But you don't have to grow up attending church (or practicing Islam or visiting the synagogue, the Gurdwara, or observing whatever religion was in your family or community) to have an attachment to something greater than you.

Giving her a name

Some people see the Universe as energy they call "Source," "Light," "Divine Being," and many other terms that conjure an ethereal vibe. They believe we are energy and after we die, we return to this same source of energy. Others view the Universe as a deeper part of themselves and use it as a way to further a connection to their soul. You may see the Universe as a flaxen-haired woman who looks like Lady Gaga riding an oversized Goldendoodle. Bottom line: The Universe is the cosmic coupling between you and what surpasses the here and now.

If you don't buy into anything beyond the present moment and the half-eaten bowl of Cheerios resting on your lap, that's okay. I gain comfort sitting in meditation and finding a part of myself that links to something greater, something I call "the Universe," you may call God, and others call Lady Gaga.

The Universe is your hype woman

The Universe is that best friend who introduces you saying, "This is Cammie. She's an amazing artist, mother, and she's super good at karaoke." And you blush responding, "I'm not *that good* at karaoke." The Universe is here to hype you up and sing your praises.

The Universe's only intention is to point you toward your purpose and true path. If you trust the Universe to guide you, life becomes easier.

It doesn't mean you stay out drinking every night, eat three pizzas, call in sick to work, and wake up saying, "the Universe has got this! Pass me a mimosa." You don't get a supporting role in this thing called *your life*. You're still the lead. You have to put in the work, set intentions, and head toward your purpose with action. But the Universe will be here … helping you hit every note.

Get your gratitude on

Gratitude is about giving up the "thank yous" on a cosmic level. It goes back to our Law of Attraction. "Like attracts like." If we say or write or think, "I'm thankful for all this money coming my way," or, "I have so much gratitude for the abundance of love in my life," the Universe says, "You're welcome. Here's some more of the good stuff." Exercising gratitude raises our vibrations and living in a high energy state is how we meet our manifestations.

Whether it's about love or money or the career you're attracting, "think thank you" and whatever you're focused on will grow with gratitude.

Mood altering bonus? It's impossible to be well acquainted with gratitude and dwell in resentment, bitterness, and self-pity. Gratitude is a quick fix to move us out of these low energy emotions. Don't just try it, believe it, feel it. Sit in meditation or quiet your mind and get your gratitude on.

Bad things happen to good meditators, too

So, what do you say to the Universe when things go sideways? Imagine you lost your job. Acceptable reflexes include: "I feel pissed off, I feel treated unfairly, I feel inept, I feel cast aside, I feel angry at the boss who fired me. I feel ___." We could keep going, right? You probably picked up my list halfway through and filled in the blanks with phrases of your own.

Negative ideas and feelings don't launch into the Universe and hex our enemies—exact opposite. We're casting spells that come right back to our door step. Remember the Law of Attraction? The Universe reads our energy and matches it. Everywhere you look, you'll see that same thread of anger and aggrieved emotions in YOUR life. Your old boss is happily rolling along, and you're choking on the negative energy you packed up and took as severance.

Reframe "losing your job" with gratitude. For example, write, or think, or say, "I am thankful I have time with my kids. I'm thankful I can go back to school. If I had stayed at that job, I wouldn't have pursued my real passion, which is teaching. I'm thankful I'm not living with that stress anymore." Lose the negative chatter and tiresome labels about this experience and make room for the high-vibe life you're creating.

Hail Mary

If a lot of this chapter sounds similar to what you were taught sitting in a pew with a Bible on your lap "God has a purpose" replaced with the word "Universe," well, it is. It's about faith and trusting that the light within you and the capacity of the almighty Universe can mastermind the life you want. It's still about belief. It's still about finding comfort in a world beyond us. And, if we're being honest, it's still a cosmic crapshoot, and we're down here hoping to Hallelujah for a big win.

One of my favorite jokes or maybe it's a parable or maybe I don't know the difference ... goes something like this:

A boxer is in the ring during a fight and he's getting pummeled, totally brutalized, punch after punch, and he looks up at God and says, "God, you've got to help me, you've got to get me out of this."

And God answers, "I will, my son, but you've got to throw a punch."

That's how it works with this Universe business. The Universe is here to help, but you've got to take a swing.

Start swinging

The Universe is patient. You can take side roads for forty years and when you're ready to find your true path, it will be there with signposts and roadmaps. It won't punish you for bad decisions and terrible jokes at a date auction. (I've heard.) Get clear about what you want and walk toward it with intention. The Universe will be there cheering you on like the congregation after a Good Friday Slam Poetry Competition. Wait ... is that not a thing?

Let's overthink it

I didn't get this from an empowerment book, lecture, or energy healing workshop. It's a fun road trip game I play with my friends to pass time between snack stops. But if you're of the overthinking variety, you'll spot some insights along the way and many glimpses of gratitude.

To get started, grab a notebook, a writing utensil, and open to a blank sheet of paper. Find a quiet spot to sit where you can overthink your thoughts. Ask yourself (or your friends) the question:

Imagine yourself at twenty-two years old, what would your twenty-two-year old self think of you right here and now?

If you're currently twenty-two, back up to sixteen years old. If you are seventy-two, start at twenty-two and jump to forty-two, then to fifty-two, and see what you come across. This is a way to measure our lessons and see how many miles we still have to travel.

For most of us, our younger selves will be grateful for many things in our life that we find easy to overlook as we get older. On the left side of your paper, list your gratitudes.

At the same time, we may wonder about detours that have left some aspirations by the side of the road. On the right side of your paper, list things you'd still like to accomplish.

Looking at your first list, note everything you have to be grateful for and take pride in your accomplishments. Now look at your second list, notice if there's anything left unachieved that you want to pick up and bring along as you continue your trip.

7 CHAPTER
OVERTHINKING POSITIVE THINKING
a dark chapter

The other day, I had a chance to put my bullshit into practice.

A friend looks at me with pain in their eyes and says, "I don't know, I'm just not happy, I'm really struggling." After talking a bit, I wade in with, "Have you tried gratitude?" I hear the words fall from my mouth, and I want to grab them and tuck them back into a time five minutes before. It feels empty, naive, and even heartless. The friend is nice about it, humoring me before we switch subjects. We quickly get into action steps—seeing a doctor, finding an antidepressant, outlining what's working in their life and what's not.

That's the truth of this work and the facts of positive thinking. It's not a panacea. You can't snap your fingers and switch your mindset. Problems won't disappear with positive thought. Ennui isn't eliminated by enlightenment.

Practical magic

There are situations where positive thinking feels like a punchline and a punch in the gut. I get it.

Throughout my life, depression is something I could access more easily than the PIN number on my ATM card. It's like "depression/anxiety" is my factory default setting, and I spent years looking for the reset button. I see people with other settings, and I wonder what it must be like to have a dial set at "cheerful," "content," or "genuinely likes camping."

Looking back, there are times I could chant every mantra and shout affirmations at the top of my lungs and it wouldn't change how I felt. I was barely making ends meet and working a job that took every ounce of my mental energy. Thankless bosses, uninspiring work, and credit card debt that neared the number of an annual salary. To add self-injury to insult, I was drinking too much so brain chemicals pinged from high to hangover to dips of depression. This wasn't a job for positive thinking. And frankly I wasn't grateful for shit.

My memories of that time are covered in a vellum-like haze as if the June Gloom in LA settled over and begged for the sunlight to break through. Much of my pain was situational, circumstantial, I had to make better choices and create stability where happiness could find its footing.

Without much fanfare or crying to the gods, I make moves in small motions. I quit a job and chose a healthier work situation. I stop drinking, I end unhealthy dating cycles, and the June Gloom begins to lift. Full disclosure, I've always been on SSRIs for my migraines. SSRIs are antidepressants and often prescribed to people with headaches. But trust me, I appreciate the overlap and bask in the benefits of a serotonin spike.

Back to the June Gloom. While things are a bit brighter, I still feel the fog. This gets me overthinking even more. I no longer have a bad job, a no-good guy, or an impaling hangover to absorb the assault of my mood. So, I pick up books (listed in the back), I listen to podcasts, I do workshops, and I start meditating. With that, everything else changes, too. The Gloom, gone. Mood, lighter.

Happiness is not something readymade. It comes from your own actions. —Dalai Lama XIV

Here's the secret: positive thinking isn't mind magic. It's equal parts action and practical advice you'd get from your nanna. I couldn't just end unhealthy dating patterns. I had to plaster the self-worth hole that led me to those relationships. It wasn't only about smarter drinking. I had to face why I acted that way to begin with. **I'd gone through the motions to get healthy, but the last thing I had to change was my mind.**

Self-help isn't an extreme sport. Start slow and make changes that feel urgent or easy. Create habits that support your well-being and stop behaviors that hurt you. Before you know it, positive thinking will feel like a well-loved habit and not at all like "bullshit."

Let's overthink it
The "P" word

Having the time and space to work on yourself is a privilege with a capital "P." It's a privilege to throw up your hands and say a job "just isn't working for you." We can't think our way out of every situation. And for many people, those situations are serious, historically unfair, or even dangerous. So where do you start if so much more needs to change than your mind?

To get started, grab a notebook, a writing utensil, and open to a blank sheet of paper. Find a quiet spot to sit where you can overthink your thoughts.

If you're in a place where circumstances feel too big to tackle, let's start with a plan. It helps you feel in control of the situation and provides a blueprint to make changes when time allows. On the lefts side of your paper, make a list of what is working in your life. Your lists may look like this:

List one: What *is* working.
I love my partner
My kids are doing well
Supportive community
My church

On the right side of your paper, make a list of what is not working.
List two: What *is not* working.
My job
My salary
My debt
My finances
My drinking
Need I go on ...?

Take time to feel grateful for the accomplishments or circumstances from list one. Now look at list two. Number your list by ease or urgency. For instance, the easiest thing may be consolidating your credit card debt to a zero percent interest card. That's one step in the right direction.

Maybe you can't take on anything right now but you can see "moving" is a top priority for you and your family. Next to "moving" write the action steps you need to get there. As you feel ready, make a plan to conquer each item from list two. It may take a few years, but knowing your action steps lessens anxiety and helps you envision the future you want to create.

Part II
Thinking
Through
The
Tough Stuff

8 CHAPTER
OVERTHINKING BODY IMAGE
slim shady

At eleven-years-old, I hid sandwiches under my bed. Not to hoard and eat later, but to dispose of and never eat anything, ever. I'd make a sandwich, tell my mom I'm eating in my room, put aforementioned sandwich under my bed, and throw it away at a future point in time. Once ... I forgot, and my sister found a moldy peanut butter and jelly tucked in my mattress. She made fun of me mercilessly. She still brings it up on occasion, "Remember how you used to hide food under your bed?" she'll say. You hide a sandwich ONE TIME, and you're a "moldy sandwich hider" the rest of your life.

As you may have knit together, I had an eating disorder in middle school and high school, anorexia to be specific. If you aren't versed on the subject, it's the one where you restrict food and calories to dangerous levels, and I excelled at it. I may have a single glass of milk for the entire day, a small cup of pudding on another, or a whole bowl of cereal if I was hungry. I hardly put a stick of Juicy Fruit in my mouth for fear of fat and calories lurking in the gummy substance. There were nights I lay in bed and my aching stomach and spinning head sent me running to the kitchen for a fistful of crackers out of fear I'd pushed things too far. To this day, I can't go to bed hungry because the late-night rumbles bring back unsettling feelings from long ago.

I remember sort of a "before and after" of my eating disorder and an awakening about my body.

Before ... a summer when I'm eleven years old, feathered naturally curly hair, crooked teeth, and a tummy still round with baby fat. Jumping in the lake and playing with boys without awareness to be self-conscious about things such as beauty or how your stomach folds over a swimsuit. At some point, I look down at my belly and think maybe this isn't "pretty." It isn't how women are supposed to look, and I should fix what seems wrong.

After ... I don't remember how it starts or its progression. I begin working out, eating less, and the effort feels empowering. During this time, life at home is messy. My mom is battling fibromyalgia, my sister is pressing the limits of her teenage angst HARD, and I hold tight to the one thing I can control, my weight.

My relationship with exercise turns obsessive and my eating non-existent. Monday through Friday, I consume around 1,000 calories for the entire week and on the weekend, I eat whatever I want. Friends and I prepare heaping plates of nachos, cookie dough, and homemade pizza. But the pain of filling a hollow stomach leaves me too weak to enjoy the menu I've been imagining. Worse is the dread of doing it all over again come Monday morning.

One night I come home from dance class and tell my parents I picked up dinner at Nonna's Café between two of my classes. Overhearing, my sister chimes in, "Nonna's is closed on Mondays." And she wasn't teasing me. She was right. I'm lying about eating. I can't remember what happened next. I don't know if I dig in, insisting Nonna's is open this particular evening, or if my parents push a plate of meatloaf toward me without another word. What I remember is it stung. Not because of punishment or embarrassment, but because my behavior isn't something I even admit to myself. I go through the motions, ducking dinner, and bowing out of breakfast, but hearing my lie caught midair and tossed back my direction brought reality to my dinner plate. This whole routine is physically and emotionally deteriorating, but I don't know how to let go. Or, I don't want to.

Things continue this way for years until one day my mom and dad sit me down and say they know I have a problem, and I'll be getting help, like tomorrow. It isn't a sensational event made for *A&E*. I don't cry, or argue, or insist I am well. I'm relieved. I've been living this way for too long, and I'm tired of the dangerous game I'm playing.

If you're wondering how this took so long, if my parents are jet-setting workaholics, and I was raised by an owl who lived in the backyard, the answer is "no." Eating disorders are like any problematic behavior, and you do what's necessary to get your fix. You eat a bite of bagel so your mom concludes you had breakfast. You say you had dinner at a friend's house. You are coming, going, and gliding through the door with the line, "I just ate." My parents didn't know what to think. I was thin to begin with and an active kid, so who's to say how much I should weigh during a time when adolescent bodies shift with our moods.

The therapist I meet during this time is a lovely woman named Lydia. Lydia is fun, easy, and bribes me with Diet Cokes to share my thoughts and tell her my feelings. Over the next few years, until I graduate high school, we meet about once a week. It isn't a drippy, tearful therapy. It's a casual, "so what's going on?" and "who's this boy you like?" conversation. But somehow, Lydia helps. Maybe too much.

When I get to college, I immediately overachieve at one university tradition—the freshman fifteen. I gain twenty pounds by the end of my first year from a steady diet of late-night pizza and Sunny Delight mixed with gas station vodka. I'm not eating normally, but at least I am eating. I don't love what I see in the mirror, but I enjoy loosening the reins I've been gripping for so long. As the semesters pass, my eating habits worsen and the weight settles in as a new part of me. I eat because I'm alone. I eat because I'm with my friends. I eat because I'm drunk. I eat because I'm hungover. I eat because I'm flunking algebra. I don't swap an addiction to restricting food for an addiction to consuming it, I simply have no idea how to eat normally because I haven't done so since I was eleven.

Houston, we have a problem

Emerging from college and entering the real world is a reentry phase worthy of NASA coordination. It's abrupt and jarring no matter who you are. College is a smog of bad habits and suddenly, you're thrust into the atmosphere of 7:30 a.m. alarms and status meetings with people who look like your parents. Late nights are traded for early morning commutes. Social circles that supported you for years evaporate overnight and adult responsibilities appear in an instant.

I am working my first job in Chicago and trying to eat well on a paycheck that hardly covers my rent. I cook meals laden with pasta, bread, and rice-rich casseroles. Being from the Midwest—this is how food looks. It's how comfort feels. And I have no other reference.

Keep in mind this is 2001 before green juice is served at fast-food restaurants and wellness influencers appear in a swipe on your phone. Those college pounds are sticking around and adding a few friends to the mix. I feel as if I'm living in someone else's body, and I don't know how to get mine back.

At a loss for how to correct my diet, I run before work, after, or on my lunch break. The rhythm of a routine makes me feel strong for the first time in years. With that comes the desire to eat better, too. I watch documentaries about the influence food plays on our health and well-being. And, eventually, I gather information I should've picked up in kindergarten. "You are what you eat. Food is fuel. Put good things in your body to get good results." I keep running and thinking about food in this new way. The college weight drops, and I finally have control of my eating. But this time, I am healthy and devoted to treating my body well.

I still operate this way when it comes to food. I eat pizza (though not at two a.m.), and I love going for Mexican food and having two baskets of chips before the food arrives, but I choose these things in moderation because I know they don't add value to my body. I don't count calories. The only time I weigh myself is at the doctor. I work out consistently because my body needs it. But a dirty little secret I keep to myself and share with you now is that I still can't see my body or even myself accurately. It's not an obsession like when I was younger, it's more of a blind spot like looking in the rearview mirror and knowing objects appear differently in reality.

Damn the Gram

I watch the same TV and consume the same social media as you and it's a hot garbage fire for our self-worth and body image. I grew up in a time when rail-thin was revered, but today's body standards aren't any easier to measure up to. You're no longer only balancing the scale of your peer group, but an entire world weighs in with their falsehoods and fake filtered realities. One scroll through our feeds and suddenly, we're an insecure eleven-year-old wondering why we don't look like the other girls.

Whether you're a size two or a size twenty, few of us get a pass on the fragileness that comes with accepting our bodies. Unfollow people and accounts who create a distorted picture of real life. Find a body-positive role model to follow. See how they live abundantly without auto-tuning their nose into a bird beak. Better yet, go dark on social media altogether. Don't fall for a myth that you need to be followed or liked or validated by anyone besides you. know. who. (It's you.)

Let's overthink it

What I've learned from life or *Lifetime* movies, is that eating disorders aren't about weight or waistlines. **An eating disorder is about seizing control in a very visible way because so much of life is outside our view. It's about focusing on one sound so you can't hear the noise around you.** If I thought about calories, counted my sit-ups, and concentrated on my next few bites, I didn't have to absorb the tension at home and might dampen the stress of adolescence.

If you've wrestled with a disorder of any kind, you know that even after you put down the drink, or pick up your fork, you still catch passing glances. To this day, I see "control" weaving in and out of my life in various ways, whether it's a need to make it to my yoga class four to five times a week or finish a work project two days ahead of schedule. At the seed of control is an illusion that nothing bad can happen if you dot every "i" and cross every last thing off a never-ending to-do list.

Managing our control settings

To get started, grab a notebook, a writing utensil, and open to a blank sheet of paper. Find a quiet spot to sit where you can overthink your thoughts.

Let's assess your relationship with control. Where are you holding tight to a thing/situation/action/person and ask yourself why?

On the left side of your paper, write your control issue. Your list could be one item or many.

Your list may look like this:

Food

My children

Money

Working out

Cleaning

Work

Continuing on the left side of your paper, ask yourself, "What would happen if I gave up a little control? Or rather, "What's the worst that could happen?"

Your edited list may look like this:

Food – I get ill from not eating well.

My children – My kids misbehave, don't get into a good college, etc.

Money – We go broke, we're homeless.

Working out – I gain weight.

Cleaning – I appear imperfect.

Work – I lose my job, everyone realizes I'm a fraud.

On the right side of your paper, try to identify the origin of your control issue, or the first time it appeared in your life. This may help uncover new core beliefs or labels which, we can work through and craft in a positive way.

On second thought

No matter how much I overthink, I don't have the answers or advice to issues as pervasive and personal as the tough stuff in this section: eating disorders, drinking, substance abuse, and much more. I can tell you my experience, but professional help is necessary. If disordered eating, alcohol, or any other subject we discuss is a problem for you or a loved one, I encourage you to utilize everything at your disposal from talk therapy to medical doctors to twelve-step programs as you find your way. Please see resources in the back for more information. I'm rooting for you.

9 CHAPTER
OVERTHINKING SELF-DOUBT
why me?

Upon graduation, I feel utterly inept to get a job in the real world. It isn't some sort of deep-seated insecurity. It's more that I'm utterly inept to get a job in the real world. I've recently moved from Missouri to Chicago and set my sights on a career in advertising mostly because of my obsession with Angela Bower from the eighty's TV hit *Who's The Boss?*

Growing up, I'd sit in my room and scratch out ideas for Pepsi and Levi commercials in a heart covered notebook while wearing oversized shoulder pads made from throw pillows and yelling at my imaginary Italian maid. Eventually, my intense love of sitcoms melds with my childhood creativity and points me in a career direction and the Windy City.

At a loss for how to enter my chosen profession, I visit a placement agency in the Chicago Loop. The lobby is a beige box of stale air with furniture tossed together in a potluck of styles. A "Teamwork" poster clings to the wall with a lone piece of Scotch Tap browning at the edges. I shift uncomfortably in my navy blue suit and thumb an "AARP" magazine from last year. At twenty-two, this is only the second time I've worn such grown-up garb. The

---

* I can't possibly explain the mismatched magic of Tony Danza and Judith Light. Please find a "Nick at Night" situation and watch this gem of '80s glory.

first was in the dressing room at Oak Park Mall where my mom purchased it for me.

An expressionless woman snakes her head around a corner, scanning a clipboard for a name. "Lindsay?" she says.

I stand and follow her into a storage closet of an office. We take seats opposite one another over a desk in disarray. Pushed to the front of the clutter is a placard that says, "The bitch stops here" with the name "Donna" underneath.

"So, what do you want to do with your life?" Donna asks, not breaking eye contact with the papers in front of her.

What a layup of a question, Donna!

I've only been planning this answer since Angela and Tony acknowledged their chemistry in season eight.

"I want to be the person who comes up with TV commercials," I say confidently. Too confidently, perhaps, for a girl who doesn't even know the name of the job title she's seeking.

Donna looks up from her papers. "'Copywriter.' You want to be a copywriter," she says as an instruction rather than a question.

"C-o-p-y-w-r-i-t-e-r." I repeat as if I'm listening to Rosetta stone.

"Do you have a portfolio?" Donna asks.

Another new word! This is turning into a fun game.

"A what?" I ask.

"A book with your writing samples in it," Donna says.

I think back to my heart covered notebook and estimate this isn't what Donna is after.

"I'm working on it," I say.

"Hmmm." Donna smirks and continues, "Can you answer phones?"

"Well, obviously," I reply.

It turns out, answering phones isn't so obvious as I take my new position at an ad agency on Michigan Avenue—as a receptionist. It isn't that the job is demeaning or beneath me, it's that it isn't. I can't manage the tasks within my job description. I drop calls as I hit the transfer button only for the angry caller to try back and rhetorically ask me how hard it is to use a phone. "There are a lot of buttons," I reply to no one's amusement. Collating copies is an escape room challenge wrapped in a geometry problem. *"What do you mean I printed 7,000 copies, but they're all upside down and backward?"* The fax machine screeches at me in its high-pitched tones, returning the message of "FAIL." Which is how I feel most days.

During one of my reviews, my manager tells me I'm not smiling enough as guests enter the lobby. And here's the thing, I smile all the time, I'm a professional smiler, people have called me "Smiley" as a less than creative nickname. Smiling is the ONE THING I CAN DO RIGHT. So, it's not that I can't handle feedback, it's that it's freaking inaccurate, and I don't like inaccuracy.

I graduated from college, moved to the big city, and I'm stalked by self-doubt. The outside world has a new pace and even its own lingo. From "EOD" to "R&D," I feel lost, left behind, and don't think I'll ever find my way.

There's no sexy *Devil Wears Prada* montage where I collate copies with a wink, send a fax without failing, and learn to blend my blush properly. I keep smiling and eventually with the help of some kind creatives,* I put together my portfolio, and get a job as a copywriter.

Imposter Syndrome

When we talk about self-doubt, there's no nastier little liar than imposter syndrome. The term "imposter syndrome or imposter phenomenon" was originated by Dr.

---

* That's what they call "copywriters and art directors" at ad agencies, "creatives." It sounds half cool, half pretentious, but it's a term and it's what they call them. Second, one of those "creatives" went on to be a serious boyfriend, a good boyfriend. The kind of boyfriend that doesn't get a whole chapter not because he wasn't a novel part of my life, but because it doesn't take a lot of overthinking to know it.

Suzanna Imes and Dr. Pauline Rose Clance in their 1978 article, "The Imposter Phenomenon in High Achieving Women: Dynamics and Therapeutic Intervention."[6] Since Imes' and Clance's publication, the definition of imposter syndrome has broadened to include almost everyone in this non-exclusive club of double doubters.

Imposter Syndrome wants to upend your self-worth and replace it with incessant insecurity.

To get clinical on you, Imposter Syndrome is a common phenomenon where a person adopts persistent feelings of insecurity and self-doubt despite past success or in relation to their current skill set. They may be highly regarded in their field or industry, yet their success doesn't line up with their self-image. They have a "blank slate mentality" when it comes to their achievements. Even though they nail the speech, develop an idea, or make the sale, they must prove themselves worthy at the start of every new task.

Imposter Syndrome can be as scary as the description above or as mild as needing a pep talk in the mirror before a meeting. But know it's there and it happens to everyone. Some of the most accomplished people in the world have leaned in to imposter syndrome, including Sheryl Sandberg, former COO of Meta.

You want to "open a boutique," or "move abroad," or "start a charity," but the whole thing is hairy and scary and anchored in self-doubt? If something pushes beyond your perimeter, imposter syndrome will make an appearance asking "are you qualified?," or "who cares what you think?," or "you serious with that outfit?."

When you set a goal, let doubt be your guide. Some of those negative labels from chapter two will beg for attention as you look above your sightline. Stretch your neck. Push past them. They are there to show us our edges and help us decide if we want to live within the framework we've built or construct something totally new.

Send in the clowns

Early on, I'm unsure of myself as a copywriter, despite receiving encouraging feedback and my ability to make mass generalizations sound believable. I'm convinced everyone around me is some sort of Oxford genius and it's only a matter of time before they sniff out my shortcomings.

It takes years and numerous jobs to prove to myself this isn't true. First, no one who works in advertising went to Oxford.[*] Second, and this is true of every industry,[**] your colleagues want you to contribute, share thoughts, and bring bagels. We sit in meetings praying someone has a pebble of a point, a shred of an idea—say anything.

As a young person, I looked to authority with intimidation until one day it hit me "No one knows what they're doing." We're all out here Live Action Role Playing our lives and hoping no one sees the props.

So, where does that leave us? Do we accept we're all a bunch of bozos and join the circus? No. Get good at what you do. Become an expert, so you can be the ringleader. Be prepared, so others look to you for answers.

You deserve to be in every room or Zoom. Think out loud, let people see the inside of your brain as you work out your reasoning. Don't be afraid to be wrong. In the end, people remember your effort rather than your errors. And yes, if you can ... always bring bagels.

"Ninety-nine percent of failures come from people who have the habit of making excuses."— George Washington Carver

Excuse me

Self-doubt wouldn't stand a chance without its whiny wingman "excuses." Excuses are defense mechanisms, self-saboteurs, covert operatives that impair us from moving beyond our current state. Most of us have our excuses holstered and ready the minute anything challenges our borders. When an opportunity arises, you produce an

---

[*] RE: Mass generalization.
[**] Bonus mass generalization.

excuse to hold you back. "I wish I had more experience. I wish I was more qualified. I wish I was a little bit taller. I wish I was a baller." You get the point. Your inner monologue is an expert at wielding excuses to protect you from potential pain. Cozying up to our excuses lessens their magnitude and allows us to see them as artificial intel instead of factual pieces of evidence we need to overthink.

I feel attacked

In advertising, self-doubt is baked into the job description to a crisp, flaky glaze and criticism is an everyday occurrence. You receive an assignment, pour an anxiety-producing portion of coffee, and hope for a creativity buzz.

Two cups in, it comes to you. It begins as a nugget that multiplies into an idea. It's energizing, fulfilling, and you're proud of your little nugget. You share it with the account manager who says, "It's good, BUT ..." And your nugget is changed ever so slightly and shown to the account supervisor. The account supervisor says, "I like it, BUT ..." And your original nugget is modified and shown to the junior client who says, "It's fine, BUT ..." And the revised nugget that you could live with is edited a smidge and shown to the senior client who says, "It will work, BUT ..." And the changed, modified, revised nugget that's not your nugget anymore goes to a focus group of people willing to spend a Tuesday evening evaluating advertising concepts, drinking Sprite out of Dixie Cups, and eating leftover Starburst from Halloween say, "We hate it. It makes us sad. The color orange is offensive." And you start over, digging for a new nugget.

If I just made a handful of advertising majors change their career trajectory, I'm sorry. I'm going to turn a corner here.

The majority of criticism isn't about us, yet we absorb the onslaught as if it's ours alone. I'm not suggesting we rationalize away every piece of negative feedback. But don't bear the brunt of other people's opinions or praise.

Whether it's advertising, an art piece you share online, or you're a CPA who does numbery tax things, be proud of your effort and trust your talent. In our LOUD and chaotic world, every voice cannot matter. Choose who gets your attention. Maybe it's a mentor and a small group of friends and family. Understand the rest is just NOISE and shut. it. off.

In my advertising job, the paycheck requires you to nod, smile, and apply feedback without flinching. What you're not required to do is take it personally.

Paying the price

For a large portion of my career, I was not paid what I was worth. Too large a portion, an embarrassingly large portion, an "I coulda-boughta-yacht"-sized portion. And for an even more red-faced, embarrassing reason. Self-doubt kept me from asking for more money. I took what was offered and said, "Thank you, sir, and I don't need more vacation days either." At times, I was paid under market for my position or even unequal to my male counterparts. It was shitty, it was unfair, but it was also my fault for letting self-doubt get the best of me.

When I began freelancing, I got real about the market, set my rate, and said "this is what I charge, no settling, no exceptions, no excuses." Pay it or don't, but my self-worth is not up for negotiation. And guess what? People paid it. A few times they said, "Would you take X?" And I either said, "No." Or, if I said, "Yes," it was because both parties made a compromise.

This isn't a weird brag about how I ruthlessly hold out for money. It's a stark reminder. If you give an inch every time, one day you'll wake up miles away from your financial goals. Know the market, ask for what you deserve, and stand up for your self-worth.

Benefit of the doubt

Right now, I feel utterly inept to claim authority and write a book. It isn't some sort of deep-seated insecurity. It's more that I'm … you get the picture. Self-doubt, imposter syndrome, negative self-talk, it's always there, bullying us the moment we get brave.

I'm not assuming you want to quit your job and become a writer. I'm guessing, suspecting, throwing my chips on the table and betting that self-doubt permeates the pivotal decisions in your life. Maybe you want to open a BBQ sauce company with your family's spicy recipe but self-doubt whispers, "Small businesses always fail." Or, maybe you want to grab the mic of stand-up comedy and self-doubt laughs, "You have to live on the coast to make it in show biz." Or, maybe you're single and want a baby and self-doubt lies, "You need a partner to be a parent."

Everything incredible thing we set out to do begins with feelings of inadequacy and a cheap navy blue suit. Let yourself feel lost, drop the call, be the joke—without a bit of uncertainty you may never find your truth.

Let's overthink it

To get started, grab a notebook, a writing utensil, and open to a blank sheet of paper. Find a quiet spot to sit where you can overthink your thoughts.

Settling into our excuses

Let's look at a goal you set out to achieve but frequently push off until later. Settle into your excuses, so when they turn up, you know it's your brain protecting you from failure and pain.

At the top of the page, list the goal you want to work through. Then, on the left side of your paper, list the excuses you tell yourself why you couldn't/shouldn't/wouldn't achieve this goal.

I'll go first. If my goal is "Write a book." A shortlist of excuses would look like this:

- I didn't go to a fancy college. All writers go to fancy colleges.
- I'm too old.

- I need to put my energy toward freelance writing that pays the bills.
- I don't have time!

Now, dismiss your excuses and replace them with a new, more potent truth. On the right side of your paper, list your truths now. For me it sounds like this:

- A lot of writers don't have a fancy education.
- I'm a better writer now than I was in my twenties.
- All of my experience has come together right now for this moment in time.

Unload your excuses (and self-doubt), ready to take action toward your goal. When you're finished, physically crumple your piece of paper, and toss it out—discarding your excuses from your overthinking brain.

Asking for a raise

Discussing salary with your boss can be altogether awkward. Going about it with a clear plan can help you enter the process with confidence. Schedule time with your boss to discuss your salary. Maybe this is your yearly review or another time you determine.

Research ahead of time

Do an extensive search using online resources such as Glassdoor and others to see what's fair for the market and your experience. You want to be paid your worth, but you also want to be equitable to your employer.

Make a list

Look back at the previous year and make a list of your accomplishments such as winning the account, managing a team, or inventing a pill that cures the ice cream headache.

Have a number in mind

After you've looked at the market and your accomplishments, know your number. Outline your accomplishments to your boss and explain that based on your performance, you desire a raise of X amount. You may want to land exactly at that number, period, no games. Or, you may want to go high and be prepared to meet in the middle. Determine your comfort level with negotiating and proceed accordingly.

Don't let the door hit you in your ass-pirations

If your boss refuses your raise, ask if there's anything you can do over the next few months to reach the desired number. For instance, "If I bring in three new accounts in the next three months, can we revisit this discussion?" Before you set your salary meeting, update your resume, do some preliminary searches online, and prepare yourself to look for a new job if necessary. That way, if you and your boss can't come to an agreement, you're confident and ready to find a job that aligns with your worth.

10 CHAPTER
OVERTHINKING FAILURE
know your hang-ups

The first time I was fired, I knew exactly what I was doing. Not in the job, of course. But the firing itself was strategic. Planned out. From the minute I enter orientation, I want nothing more than to be dismissed, sacked, tossed out on my tuchus.

In college, my friends and I decide to try our hands at the hot business of cold calling. In 1998, half the campus of Missouri State University (shout-out Bears) work at a nearby MCI call center. If you haven't kept up with the sexy telecommunications wars, MCI is now a part of Verizon. Rumor has it, MCI pays seven dollars an hour* plus commission on your sales, and there are kids taking home a thousand dollars a week at this racket. "How hard can it be?" we thought. In real life, we talk on the phone all the time and sometimes people hung up on us.

Corporate-ish America

We enter the MCI campus and tumble into a sprawling maze of featureless cubes and watercooler enthusiasm. Freezing, unmoving air pipes through the halls like a chintzy Vegas casino. PowerPoint signage guides us to "Team Rhino" or "Team Tiger" as if we're thrust back into

---

* If you're trying to do a complex inflation rate in your head, it was about two dollars over minimum wage at the time.

nursery school but this time without naptime or the blind hope of a four-year-old.

Forward-thinking managers split us up, so we're seated miles across the expansive warehouse space. We've transitioned from college gossip to chit chat with coworkers twice our age about alimony payments and sons fresh out of rehab. At the close of each sale, an over-energy-drinked manager rings a bell and runs the aisles, high-fiving this ragtag group of college kids and down-on-their-luck divorcees.

Right away, my friend, Emily, excels at our new job to *Wolf of Wall Street* proportions. She's ringing bells and bringing home commission checks that could pay our tuition. Meanwhile, my friend, Trisha, and I figure out how to surpass the sales queue and call each other between pods. We chat about hangovers and which free snacks to eat on our fifteen-minute break. MCI must have an algorithm for hiring college students. For every "Lindsay" consuming her body weight in gummy worms, there's an "Emily," selling long distance packages like an auctioneer at the Springfield, Missouri county fair.

Soon, we're introduced to a phrase which runs counter to my very essence "sales quota." As off-putting as I find the term, I'd found my out game.

At MCI, you're given two months to reach "quota," and in that time, if you aren't slinging long distance as if it's your calling, you're fired. I plan to go to work with my best friends, consuming free snacks, and collecting my seven dollars an hour, and after sixty days, I'll return to my normal college student life of eating processed sugar without getting paid for it.

After switching my parents, grandmother, and signing up for a landline* myself, I reach my capacity for high pressure sales. I call numbers as they appear in queue and say, "Hi, this is Lindsay from MCI, can I talk to you

---

* "Landlines" are these things we had in the '90's. Imagine if your cell phone was leashed to a wall and you couldn't do a TikTok dance while you talked on the phone.

about your long-distance* coverage?" And you know what happens next because you do the same three things when faced with a cold call. 1- They hang up. 2- They politely hang up saying, "I'm sorry, now is not a good time." 3- They get mad and hang up saying, "Never call me again, it's so rude to call in the middle of dinner." Everyone is always "in the middle of dinner" as if it's the 1950s and you stumbled onto the set of *Leave it to Beaver*.

The only technique I employ with any success is "self-deprecating sales." If a caller stays on the line long enough to let me speak, I say, "Look, I hate myself for doing this. I always hang up on people like me, too, but will you please talk to me while my manager walks by? He's hopped up on Red Bull, and I can't handle the fist-bumping today." Usually, a nice woman tells me about her daughter who's in college, or a man laughs and talks about the worst job he ever had working on a fishing boat.

Finally, my apathy pays off, and I'm fired with a full tummy and a plump bank account. Or, the other way around, both are accurate. But I also leave with a lesson I'll take throughout my life.

Opportunity calling

Every failure and misstep points us in a more finite direction toward our purpose. At MCI, I learned I'm not good at sales, and I probably never will be. It's not an area I want to place my energy or effort. Emily? Sales was her thing and she went on to be incredible at it after college. Go, Emily!**

One-trick pony

You may be a salesperson with no desire to understand design or a design person who can't sell your work. No apologies. I say this to you with no shame. I'm a

---

* "Long distance" is something people used to get really worked up about. There were "long distance wars" about which company gave you the best rate. And sometimes your parents would yell at you while you were on your landline*, "That better not be long distance!" It sounds exciting, but it really wasn't.

** Trisha is great, too. Geez, you guys are so nosy.

good writer, I'm decent at yoga, and I'm terrible at everything else. Hanging a picture on a wall? I'd lose a thumb. Doing laundry? My shirts don't stand a chance. Assembling IKEA furniture? *What do I look like, a magician?*

You don't need to be everything, you don't even need to be a lot of things—focus on what you love, be unapologetic about what you don't, and be damn good at what you do.

There will always be a designer to help you create a website for your business or an accountant ready to manage your books. (Or, a dad to hang a picture on your wall.) Find your talents, point toward your passions, and head maniacally in that direction.

Greetings from nowhere

If pressed, I could fire off no fewer than fifty-seven ways to say "Happy Birthday." You see, in my thirties, along with a partner, I started a greeting card company. Imagine the money I must've made from this fresh and innovative industry! Why am I even talking to you and not on a private island with other visionaries making paper fans out of hundred dollar bills? Ha. Ha. Ha. No, this part isn't about revolutionizing a waning profession. It's about knowing nothing and learning everything. It's about using failure as a pathfinder to your purpose.

"To succeed in life, you need two things, ignorance and confidence"—Mark Twain

At this point in my career, I'm in New York, and I've been writing ad copy for years at various agencies. Lately, "Sign up for Zero Percent APR" and "Book Your Travel Now. No Change Fee" are the most winning things coming out of my mouth, or laptop, or however you want to see it. I pine for the freedom to express myself, and I decide to do it on a 4x5 piece of paper.

Along with my partner, we work on idea after idea for our greeting cards. We name the company, acquire a business license, and print our first run of cards at $5.00 per piece.

So, let me break that down for you. If I was on *Shark Tank*, I'd tell Mark Cuban and the rest of the swarming prey that it cost me $5.00 to print each card because we chose the fanciest paper in all the land. Paper so substantial you could use it to board your house during a hurricane if you found yourself in such a bind. Then, I would explain, at the $5.00 *price point* (a word I had just learned), we need to charge a wholesaler (store owner) $10.00 per card. So, the consumer (you) would end up pulling out a twenty dollar bill in-store for a folded piece of paper that says "Hope your Birthday is the tits." *And ...* shark attack.

Quippy ways to say "get well" may have been my thing, but calculating price margins was NOT. Things continued this way for years. Drops of creative fulfillment paired with floods of reality. Your New York business taxes cost more than your fanny-pack-size apartment. The joy of a big box retailer acquiring your cards followed by a royalty check for $4.12.

Needless to say, the greeting card company didn't become the Hallmarkyen Empire I had in my mind. Maybe for my lack of business acumen or because even my grandmother sent me an e-card for my birthday. I retooled and refocused my life on advertising and other types of writing. I learned from it, and I let it go.

Making lemonade

The stories I tell in this book are about situations or things that did NOT work out. I'm not regaling you with tales of my high achieving high wire acts. If that's what you're after, Jeff Bezos's book goes on sale soon. Granted, Bezos has more bragging rights than me, but over the years, I learned "our losses carry the lessons." *Or, as the internet would say, "success is cool, but have you tried utter defeat"?*

You see, failure comes with a fancy farewell gift. Something you can't buy online or learn in college. In fact, it's a "win" you only get for losing. Failure spurs grit —a Kevlar vest of character that makes you more bulletproof when you take your next shot. You know where you fall short. Where you stand out. And where you need to calculate paper costs.

Don't be afraid to fail. To pick up the phone and hear, "please never call me again." To start a business with a hearty helping of sarcasm and not much else. To take the test. To run for office. To start a movement. To share your voice. To ask for more. To gather your grit. To grow your self-worth. And maybe even make a gillion dollars like that f&%ing boss, Jeff Bezos.

Let's overthink it

Okay wait, if we don't overthink failure, we're doomed to repeat it. History, ya know? Yes and no. When it comes to failure, we can't lug it around, allowing it to tug hard on our self-worth. So, an exercise I adapted during this time is the fifteen-minute overthinking session. It allows us to soak up some of that much-loved analysis without drowning ourselves in the process.

Let's say a situation screams for scrutiny—an account is lost, a project implodes, or a business fails. I'll take fifteen minutes to appreciate what went wrong, see how I'd act differently in the future, accept ownership, and move on. I will *"pick it up and put it down."* I won't carry failure for the next month and feel its weight in disproportion to the event.

To get started, grab a notebook, a writing utensil, and open to a blank sheet of paper. Find a quiet spot to sit where you can overthink your thoughts. Set the timer on your phone for fifteen minutes. Make this exercise as simple or complex as you like. Use these minutes for a meditation on a specific failure or examine your thoughts on paper.

At the top of the page, jot down a failure you're working through. For example, "My business failed."

On the left side of your paper, write everything that went wrong, regardless of fault of finger-pointing. For example, "I miscalculated paper cost."

On the right side, observe how you'd proceed differently in the future. For example, "I'd do more upfront research before entering a specific sector of business." Take the fifteen minutes to write anything and everything you want to say to yourself.

When your time ends, look over your list and throw it away. No good comes from reliving an event that lowers your self-worth. Existing in the state of suffering or a past condition of sadness affects our physical and mental health. Give pain and failure its 15 minutes, stop the clock—and your overthinking.

Brief Thoughts

Discarded greeting card lines

+ It's YOUR DAY to be the center of attention.
Opposed to other days when you're just being a narcissist.
Happy Birthday

+ Before I met you, I was really into assholes.
Okay, that sounded different in my head ...
Happy Anniversary

+ You don't look a year older.
Seriously, we all think you had work done.
Happy Birthday.

+ You may not be the best boyfriend ...
Oh, that was it.
Happy Valentine's Day.

+ If the last political season has taught me
anything about friendship ...
It's that you're wrong.
Happy Birthday!

11 CHAPTER
OVERTHINKING AND DRINKING
zero tolerance

I'm not so much a high-functioning alcoholic as I am a low-functioning social drinker. Everyone has a different tolerance for alcohol and mine is painfully low. You could have two drinks and operate a forklift, and when I have two drinks, I can't lift my fork. It's something I had to come to terms with in my thirties. Shut'er down. Last call. Tab's closed.

In high school, I have a swig here or a beer there, but I don't do any heavyweight drinking until college. For an introvert who's more comfortable with books than bars, alcohol is the antidote for the new sprint of social interactions. Pre-party shots roll into late-night "after bars" and you float on the fumes of Finlandia until morning. I often drink at whatever pace the night or my friend group demands. My hangovers are wicked and the blackouts, worse. Limits are never learned, and I carry that behavior with me as a graduation gift.

Out of college, I don't drink as often, but when I do, my poor tolerance surges back like a recently tapped keg. After a handful of drinks, I struggle to remember the night before and the following day, I puzzle together memories like Guy Pearce with a stack of Polaroids. It's terrifying, shameful, and embarrassing—even if nothing of note happens.

But one night something does. I am living in New York enjoying a typical night with friends. Cheers, drink, slur, repeat. I wake up the next morning with a gaping hole where half the night should live. The last thing I remember the sun has only started to dim, but my faculties are out like a light.

After that, it's only pieces and pictures. The face of a man I don't know leaning over me. The flare of a flashlight passing over my eyes like headlights on a highway. And pitch granite blackness. That was it. I can't recall anything else. I speak to a friend who was with me the night before, and she assures me all is well. It was a fun, boozy night, and I left the group to look for a cab as the night ended. Now, I'm home safe, and I shouldn't overthink it.

A few days later, my anxiety-hangover begins to wane, and I return to my apartment with an armful of groceries. As I head inside a neighbor stops me. She's a young woman in her twenties who frequently sits outside smoking on our stoop. Before today, we've never exchanged more than a cordial head nod.

"Are you okay?" my neighbor asks.

"Oh, hi. Um, yeah, why?" I reply.

"You don't remember, do you?" she says. Nothing rushes back to me, but I know she's about to tell me something I don't want to hear.

"You were pretty out of it the other night," my neighbor says, stomping her cigarette into the pavement.

"I came outside to smoke, and you were passed out in a cab. Driver was trying to wake you up, flashlight in the eye, the whole thing." she continues.

I look at my feet.

"I showed him where you lived. We carried you to your apartment," she says.

I mumble "thank you" or maybe "I'm sorry."

If I'm being honest, I don't know what I said. I may have laughed it off as I hurried inside.

If you're trying to add up those events (like I did), it may have unraveled like this. I left my friends and got in a cab. I gave the driver my cross streets and passed out after telling him my life story and texting two to three ex-boyfriends. When we pulled up to my address, he turned around to find a girl TKO'd without a fight. Everything he has to deal with in a day—traffic, rude passengers, city tumult. And this ... this is how he ends his night?

I know ... I hated myself, too. But more than that, I hated how little I cared to put myself in a position where maximum bodily harm could've found me. That night it didn't. That night, a few kind people went out of their way to make sure a girl they didn't know got home safely.

A few weeks later, I saw my therapist and exclaimed, "I'm obviously not an alcoholic," before launching into current events. After listening attentively to this story and other mishaps over the years, she said gently, **"You can have a problem with alcohol without being an alcoholic."** That hit like a straight up martini on a lunch of Baked Lays.

Textbook definitions, online quizzes, and Meg Ryan in her only dramatic role[*] of the '90s assured me I didn't have a problem. I never drank alone. I'd go weeks without a sip. I didn't even like the taste. But realizing alcohol may not suit your life, your personality, and could become problematic? That was an *ahhh* to the freaking *haaa* for me.

I took a hard look in the mirror and a glance at my drinking past. The reality is, *I wasn't in control.* I'd begin a night out thinking, "Well, anything can happen!" That's a fun motto for Mardi Gras but not so much for a Tuesday work dinner.

I catalogued all the times I nuked relationships or acted in a way that tanked my self-worth and without fail—alcohol was at the helm. There I was ... fighting against the current to win this self-love game, yet refusing to remove

---

[*] *When a Man Loves a Woman.* Meg was the woman. Andy Garcia, the man. Great movie.

the one thing that kept pulling me under like that girl in the first scene of *JAWS*.

I wish I could tell you I never drank again, but that's not true. I didn't drink for a long time. And a few years later, I made a deal with myself to only drink on special occasions and in situations I felt safe. Even then, I had to trust that one drink didn't morph into six, and I wouldn't wake up with a flashlight in my face.

Pseudo sober

Choosing to be on the sober side of things is physically gratifying and socially interesting. On a rare occasion, I have a drink, but on the whole, I choose to live without alcohol. There's a word for it now. They call it "sober curious," which sounds like something everyone tries "just once" in college. For me, it's the right choice. I don't want the fog of the night before rolling in the next morning like the beginning of a "Dateline Special." The aches of too much alcohol are pains I can live without.

The hard part is the beginning. At first, your friends won't understand your new way of being. In time, it becomes a known fact. "Oh, she doesn't drink," they say to the waiter before he can even hand over the wine list. It goes without mentioning after a while, and you don't have to explain it. But at first, you do. You have to tell every person you ever happied-your-hour with that things are different now. You have to say, "I'm just not drinking tonight." Or, "I have a big meeting tomorrow." Or lie, "I had too much last night." It's bizarre, right? We invent excuses for why we chose a healthier lifestyle because the ritual of drinking is held as hero in our culture.

I don't go through the theatrics anymore. I say, "I'm not much of a drinker." And I leave it there. Without further explanation. No excuses necessary.

Owning your "oops"

I beat myself up for a long time about the way I acted with my drinking. But I needed to own it, accept it, and forgive myself. In the beginning, I took time each month to reflect on how far I'd come. *"Wow, I drank Diet Coke during a four-hour happy hour and actually had fun."* I chose to be proud of my progress rather than looking back and shrinking small into regret. You can't practice self-love and overflow your self-worth until you forgive yourself and stop replaying mistakes from your past.

Put the "u" in trust

Over the years there were habits I aimed to quit—drinking, bad relationship patterns, not showing up for others. I lied aloud saying, "Oh, it was just a bad night," or "I'll do better next time." I'd make a promise to the person in the mirror and break it like a glow stick at a rave. Afterward, I not only carried the consequence of my actions, but every stumble sliced at my self-worth.

The trust you build with yourself is more meaningful than any other relationship. Whether you're preaching to the choir or mumbling to your inner monologue, your words have weight. If you decide to quit a behavior or begin a routine—follow through for YOU. Behave in a way that's consistent and show up for yourself before anyone else.

Baby steps

If you wake up on the wrong side of a night, it can feel like you'll never be right again. Focus on "the next step" to help take positive action without becoming overwhelmed with the marathon of decisions in front of you.

You can't go back and change the beginning but you can start where you are right now and change the ending.—C.S. Lewis

In the drinking example, maybe the next step is a bit of exercise to make you feel better. Focus on that step and that step only, no overthinking. The next step after that is eating something healthy. And the next step after that is a good night's sleep because your body needs it.

If you find it helpful, write the five steps you need to address for that week. Focus on your "five step list," no overthinking beyond that. Tackle your "five step list" for as many weeks as you need. Little by little, these small steps lead to higher ground where you can handle larger decisions and bigger life changes.

The hard stuff

Recently, I shared this chapter with a friend and she shook her head saying, "I had a night almost exactly like that." My story is more ordinary than outrageous and that's what we need to overthink.

We assume unnatural postures under the premise of having a good time, chasing the guy, or being the life of the party. Alcoholic or problem drinker, sober or pseudo sober, the label doesn't matter. I was recklessly toying with common sense and, as women, we don't have the luxury to be this careless. It's up to us to know our limits, mamma bear our well-being, and tuck ourselves in at the end of the night.

Let's overthink it

To get started, grab a notebook, a writing utensil, and open to a blank sheet of paper. Find a quiet spot to sit where you can overthink your thoughts.

On the left side of the paper, write a behavior you're working through: "smoking, drinking, gambling, too much social media, etc."

On the right side of the paper, write a gratitude(s) that comes with ceasing that behavior, "I feel clear headed in the morning. I have more energy, etc."

At the bottom of the paper, jot down a few "go-to" activities to replace the behavior you're trying to leave behind.

Your list may look like this:

If I want a drink or a cigarette, I will:

Work out

Walk my dog

Go for a hike

Meditate or journal
Cook or meal prep for the week
Call a friend

These activities are personal to your life, and my list may be way off your course of interests. Create a list that motivates and inspires you. Keep these activities top of mind, so you know how to curb the urge.

Why ask why

If you've been close to a person with a substance abuse disorder, you know this much—you can't be someone's reason for quitting. Everyone has to find their "why" and do it for themselves. If you're trying to quit a behavior, find your "why." Maybe it's "for your son." Or, "this is for my self-worth." Or, "I'll never make partner if I continue. This is for my career." Choose an object that represents your reason for quitting and keep it nearby. Find your "why" and hold tight.

12 CHAPTER
OVERTHINKING SHAME
hindsight in 2020

I should tell you where we are in the world as I write this. You and I were likely doing the same thing ... sitting in our underwear, watching *Tiger King*, planning a mock wedding to our dog(just me?). You may have guessed, I'm writing this during the delicate and isolating times of the Coronavirus in 2020.

As I was busy overthinking my thoughts, the world gave me so much more to contemplate.

Enter the summer of 2020 and the murders of George Floyd, Breonna Taylor, Ahmaud Arbery, and many others outside the headlines, which signals a call-to-action for Black Lives Matter. I'm going to be honest, if these events hadn't happened, the following subjects would be far from my mind. Race and privilege isn't something I overthought. *I'm a good person. Racism is over, right? Spotify play, Beyoncé on repeat!* Translation: I didn't overthink what America was like for people who weren't like me.

Then, I see a post on Instagram that says, "As white people, we need to stop being defensive about racism." My first thought: *Of course, I'm not racist. Don't be ridiculous, Instagram.* Scroll. Scroll. Scroll. My second thought? *Whitney Houston.* Now, let me back up.

When I began writing greeting cards, I was composing what *I thought* were one-liner jokes (debatable,

I'm sure). I have a series of cards you give to a girlfriend "just because" or "to make her smile." For instance, one card said, "I'm sorry you slept with that guy who made you cry." You know, Shakespeare-level shit. Well, another card said, "Next time you think about dating the bad boy, consider Whitney Houston. That's all I'm going to say..."

This is two years before Whitney tragically passed. During the time, unfortunately, Whitney is fodder for every late-night host and comedian on TV. My line isn't some sort of subversive jolt, it's derivative, lazy, and not funny at all. It's meant to be about dating the wrong guy, Bobby Brown. All of my writing back then is about dating the wrong guy, because I was about as profound as a BuzzFeed quiz.

In 2012,* Whitney dies, and I'm devastated along with the rest of the world. Beyond sadness, I feel a heavy amount of shame for making a joke at the tragic turn her life had taken. As a woman, I'm embarrassed. If anyone understands how a guy can blindside your judgment and make you act in ways beyond yourself, it's me. I jumped on a trend of finger pointing and laughing at another woman's misfortune. But, if I'm being honest, that was the edge of my reflection. I didn't have more perspective to see beyond that. And after a while... I forgot about the card. I forgot about the shame. I forgot about Whitney.

This is one of those experiences you learn from in intervals, washing over you at different times with new lessons and awakened guilt. In the light of 2020, and the overthinking that comes with it, the shame rushes back, but this time with a framework I didn't have before.

My actions mocked a Black woman who fell victim to drugs and continued a stereotype of Black culture that is unfair and oppressive. There was a reason comedians at the time and I, felt we could so casually make fun of Whitney. She was a woman. She was Black. She was fair game. "Holy shit, who am I?" I think. I try to rationalize how my

---

* The card is pulled from circulation.

situation is different. It was meant as a little joke, and again, how, "I am one of the good ones." But, I can't get there ... I have to accept that in this case, *I am not*. All of the injustice that got us to June of 2020, major missteps and *little jokes*, it all played a part, and I played my part, too.

Shortly after this, I turn on a documentary about Whitney's life. In interview after interview, her family talks about the hurt they felt and the hills she climbed to get sober. Again, I feel ashamed that I hadn't seen her with the compassion she deserved. Instead, I made her pain a punchline.

Let's overthink it

This exercise is about working through shame not racism or oppression because those conversations are not mine to enter or adopt without care or proper education.

The shame game

What we know about shame from the world of self-help is that it thrives in darkness. Many times we lock away shameful thoughts and don't even admit them to ourselves for fear of what they may mean about who we are.

To get started, grab a notebook, a writing utensil, and open to a blank sheet of paper. Find a quiet spot to sit where you can overthink your thoughts.

As you see in this chapter, some of our labels aren't easy to face in the light of day. Let's look back at your negative labels from chapter two. Do any of these labels carry an element of shame? If so, why? What is the shameful story you tell yourself associated with this label? Or, what is a shameful story from your past that you carry?

For example, on your list, you have the label, "broke." It comes from a lifetime of financial trials and filing for bankruptcy after college. Don't worry, you don't need to go Live on Instagram to bring your label to light.

Step one: Understand the origin of your label and your shame. When did it first appear in your life?

Step two: Can you see that label or element of shame showing up in other ways? You feel "poor" or "broke" around your partner's well-to-do family. List all instances this shame appears.

Step three: Find a new word or phrase to replace your label of "broke." EX: "I am smart with money and live in abundance." Sit in meditation and imagine yourself right out of college when this shame occurred. Now, see yourself moving from this state of "broke" into a new period of abundance. Recite the mantra you landed on "I am smart with money." Do this for a number of days or weeks until it feels like your new story.

Resolution: A few things may happen as you work through this exercise. You realize "I am broke" doesn't feel true to who you are now. Or, maybe you see "broke" is a part of your story but doesn't define you as a person.

We are complex human beings with bankruptcies, break-ups, and breakdowns in judgement. We don't have to be perfect to love ourselves. In fact, I'd advise against it. We need to own our mistakes, accept who we are, and do better the next time. The capacity to learn and change is what keeps us overthinking and striving toward a better version of ourselves.

PART III
THINKING
THROUGH
RELATIONSHIP
BUSINESS

13 CHAPTER
OVERTHINKING TYPE
tall, dark, & unavailable

Growing up, the shorts my dad wears to run around our neighborhood becomes the stuff of legend. Even now, thirty years later, I'll be in a conversation with a childhood friend, and they'll say, "Remember your dad's electric orange shorts?"

My friends give my dad the nickname "Baywatch' Bob" because he's unusually fit and, as previously stated, runs around bare-chested aka David Hasselhoff. I take up jogging so I can go with him. A- Because I adore my dad. B- He's slow. He doesn't really run, he sort of struts as if Fonzie is speed walking at the mall.

I have many fond memories of a living room of family and friends and my dad entertaining like an Italian Bob Hope on a USO tour. All of my dad's stories are animated and acted out like a competitive game of charades. Jokes are effective communication in my household and sarcasm our love language.

My dad isn't just a slow-running comedian in short shorts. He's also an incredibly sensitive, kind, supportive, generous, sit-down-at-the-table and asks, "How do you really feel about things?" kind of guy. We're talking an '80s sitcom-type dad. Paging Jason Seaver …

Type casting

After self-helping for years and dating for longer, I noticed there are two ways we create our type. When we understand our type, we're free to choose partners from a place of clarity, not insecurities, negative labels, or inherited patterns from our past.

Type one: Main character energy

Thanks to my dad, we skimmed type one—choosing a mate from childhood influences. **Whether it's a father, mother, sibling, or first love, when you look for a partner, you pursue traits of a familiar figure.** These traits can be terrific or not so noteworthy, but they send us on a search, sometimes dating the same *type* as we attempt to find a person who fits the part.

Time and again, you choose a partner with all the personality and no full-time job. Why? Because it reminds you of a type you cast long ago (a father, mother, the one who broke your heart). It's cozy, comfortable, and mostly, it feels like home.

When you look at your type, who are they besides tall, brown-eyed guys in Patagonia pullovers? Are they temperamental? Aloof? Avoidant of intimacy? Where do your past partners begin to cross over and can you trace those attributes back to an original character in your past?

Unfortunately, my mold for men wasn't an exact replica of my upbringing. It was like a poorly produced copy at Madame Tussauds. *Is that David Beckham or Macaulay Culkin?* My brain imprinted certain things but overlooked others, and I landed on a mishmash of characteristics that didn't add up to healthy relationships.

The partners I picked needed to fill as much space as my dad. Be as funny, be as charming, "be as big as Bob." It was a tall order that steered me away from quiet, shy guys and straight to arrogant men without the sensitivity and kindness of my dad. Men who were overly cocky and dependent on drugs and alcohol. Guys with LOADS of personality and no appetite for intimacy. Others who could take over a room but had zero space in their life for a relationship. The reason they were "my type" hit hard on three key likenesses. They were "attractive, confident, and unavailable for one reason or another." This is what I call our "Hot Starters."

Hot Starters are the top three things that pull you in and blind you to the rest of your potential partner's true self. Your Hot Starters keep you from seeing your date's faults or escort you away from the right person who doesn't match your high hot three.

My friend, Denise, consistently dated guys who played lacrosse, graduated from an East Coast school, and worked in finance. Every. Damn. Time. We were well out of college, so choosing a guy based on sport made as much sense as selecting a life partner because they both love chocolate chip ice cream. It's cool, sure, but it doesn't have much substance.

One night, Denise was reeling from a breakup with a lacrosse guy and chatting with a friend at a bar. Up walks a sweet, smart (SCIENTIST!) to ask for her number. She gave it to him, mostly to make him go away. At the time, she told me the story in passing, "Oh, yeah, and this guy asked for my number. I'm sure I won't go out with him. He's not *my type*." As is a scientist's nature, he persisted, and she accepted a date. And guess what? Denise had never been so surprised in all her life. Here she was playing games with lacrosse guys while the scientist took her on thoughtful picnics and readily offered commitment. Happily ever after ensued and Denise and the scientist recently had their second baby. What would've happened if she hadn't experimented with her type and given the scientist a chance?

If you can't see yourself with anyone besides a blue-eyed Brazilian—I love that for you. But, own your type so it doesn't own you. Know where those attributes originate. Are they traits that feed into a healthy relationship, or are you locked into "angry, rejecting, and cheap" because of something you picked up in preschool and should've put down a long time ago?

Type two: Cruise Control

"If this is where it has to happen, then this… is where it has to happen." In this scene from Jerry Maguire, Tom Cruise storms into the living room and tells "normal girl," yet totally gorgeous, Renee Zellweger, "You complete me," casting a line for us to quote for 30 years and a romance bar set so high, Tom could never see over it.

Beyond that, the writers gave us a complimentary lesson in how our brains select partners. We look for others to fill the spaces we fall short. Or, *believe* we fall short.

For example, you often date people with power or status. Looking back at your negative labels, you see "weak or small." Perhaps, a core belief lingers around "I will never get ahead," because you grew up in a family where a parent deemed your dreams impossible.

So, big deal. Opposites attract, right? If you've done the work, and you find the Yin to your Bowen Yang, of course, complete each other. Tom's lingo loses the plot if we expect a partner to fill a chasm of unresolved issues and insecurities rather than going for growth on our own.

Complete yourself first, and find a partner that's the whole damn deal.

If we're choosing people based on what's lacking in ourselves, we're not using the best picker possible. Let's say you use your negative label "unattractive" to pilot your dating life. For you—love is not blind. Leading with your label, you don't see these hotties are also, "selfish, callous, and unfaithful." Or, you do, but only after eight months and an entire tank of self-worth. "How did I miss that?" you wonder aloud while watching *Bachelor in Paradise*. Wonder not, friends. You picked a partner to fill a void of insecurity rather than working through your past and presenting your best self to the world.

Clear-eyed girl

Once you know your type, dating becomes different. I would meet and man and think, "Well, he has my Hot Starters, I can see that. He's handsome, he's confident, but is he a good person? Does he want commitment? How many times did he call the waiter "bro"? Now, I look for the essential attributes instead of the Hot Starters that get us in the door and hook us for the first few dates (or years). For me, "attractive and confident" needed to move way down the list. They are "nice to haves," but they aren't first-round draft picks when it comes to lifelong happiness. As for my number three, "unavailable." Yeah, we'll get to that as we roll through this Relationship Business.

Foxymoron

It's not only the shorts that get people talking about my dad. Friends say, "How can you have such a solid father figure and such a crap dating history?" These are good friends, best friends, the kind of friends who would break into my house and delete the search history on my laptop if I went missing, so the news headline wasn't "obsessively googled pictures of Shih Tzus right before disappearance." *Those kind of friends.* Casual acquaintances don't prod so painfully into your psyche.

I've explained a bit in this chapter—the "how it could happen" of it all. But the truth is, I don't know. A lot has to do with (you guessed it) self-worth, and not feeling deserving of a partner who treated me well. My parents treated me well—good, sitcom-level great. But strangers? Dates? I couldn't expect such decency from every person to part my path. But here's the thing. Yes, I could. Yes, you can.

Maybe your type erupts into the living room dropping lines like Eminem[*] in a rap battle. Or, maybe you only choose partners with red hair and one green eye. Again, I love that for you. Understand your type and why you pick 'em, so the grandest gesture is toward your self-worth.

---

[*] Is there a more current reference? Sure. Do I know who it is? Nope.

Let's overthink it

To get started, grab a notebook, a writing utensil, and open to a blank sheet of paper. Find a quiet spot to sit where you can overthink your thoughts.

Hot starters

What are your Hot Starters—the top three things that pique your interest in a partner? These may be easy to identify or take an archeological dig. If they don't jump out immediately, look at your last few relationships or dates. What are the top three things that stand out? They can be a mix of positive and not so positive attributes. Be honest in your evaluation to identify what's pulling from your past.

Before you narrow to your three Hot Starters, your list of longer traits may look like this:

Funny
Smart
Musical
Successful
Smug
Wants kids
Clingy
Doesn't want kids
Well-traveled
Fashionable
Cheap
Quirky
Jobless
Ambitious
Artsy
Aloof/Avoidant
Bad with money
Cruel
Wealthy
Liberal

Conservative
Addicted to pyramid schemes
Independent-minded
Attractive
Vain

After you examine your list, narrow to your top three Hot Starters. Your final list may look like this:
Smart
Successful
Aloof

Looking at your list of traits, can you see their origin? Does the list remind you of your first boyfriend, your mom/dad/brother's best friend? Our type can come from any significant relationship from childhood. Acknowledging how we choose our type ensures we're falling for a person rather than a pattern. What's connecting from your past and halting you from building a healthy relationship in your present?

Projected partner

Before we go further, let's make a list of what we're looking for in a partner. Remember, the Universe listens to our words and our actions. So be clear about what you want and act accordingly to attract this person. Go ahead and list everything you desire in a partner now. This isn't about becoming picky or impossible to please, it's about putting on paper what's important and walking away from empty attributes that have yet to deliver happiness to your life.

Hot edit

Most of us look at our Hot Starters and recognize we need a revision. Look at your Projected Partner list and select three traits to use going forward. These will become your new Hot Starters.

Keeping our example list going, maybe our edited list looks like this:
Smart

Successful

~~Aloof~~

Good communicator

On second thought

Many relationship experts take this overthinking further, explaining we choose partners in order to heal a wound from childhood. If this idea feels relevant to your experience, look for books, TED Talks, or podcasts from Esther Perel or Helen Fisher, PhD. Both women are renowned experts who can guide you through relationships, psychology, and the neuroscience of mating.

14 CHAPTER
OVERTHINKING DATING
self-love, game, set, match

The room looks as if it's been dunked in buttercream icing and run through a "noir" filter on your iPhone: white furniture, vanilla-colored carpet, wispy translucent drapes, and black and white pictures of couples intertwined in moments of intimacy. I'm sitting in an office suite in downtown Chicago meeting with a matchmaking company. I don't know this part yet, but the setup of the service is as follows. The women pay zero dinero to find a mate and the men fork over a large fee to flip through a catalog and select a mate as if shopping for socks at J. Crew.

I can't be sure how I got here. It was the Brown Line and two quick stops on a Red Line transfer. But before that … it must've been one more "Save-the-Date" in my mailbox and another spasm of "you're thirty-six and single" that led me to a link I saw online, which took me to a questionnaire, and now, here I am looking at a woman named Bethany tell me the best place in town to get a bikini wax. Is this her version of small talk, or is it somehow related to finding my soulmate? I can't tell yet.

Bethany is in her twenties, and looks as if her best friends are named "Gigi" and "Kendall." This isn't who I want telling me, "dating over thirty-five is hard." I want a woman who's buried three husbands just for the fun of it and says stuff like, "You're not going to like him all of the time, or even some of the time, or maybe *ever*, but that's love, doll," as she ashes a Parliament Light into a cactus. That's solid advice I can work with, not a YELP review about a wax salon named "The Full Spread."

Bethany runs through a few standard interview questions, pausing now and then to laugh at a text, "Oh sorry, Kyle's such an asshole," Bethany says. She continues, "What kind of guys do you like?, What do you want out of a relationship?, and How would you describe yourself?" I see the questions and my answers are merely decoys as Bethany sums me up by an unseen indicator. But I reply anyway, "Funny, a life partner, like Amy Schumer* who's uncomfortable talking about her vagina." Bethany picks up the phone on her desk and chirps into the receiver, "Send in the girls."

A few seconds later, five other Bethanys slither into the room and line up like the end of Victoria's creepiest fashion show. Bethany motions in my direction, "She's cute, right?" The girls give a dead-eyed nod of affirmation. "Would you mind taking off your jacket and standing up?" Bethany asks. *Context:* It's May, and I'm wearing a thin leather jacket. I'm not cocooned in an oversized North Face as is customary in Chicago nine months of the year. Regardless, I comply, removing my jacket and standing up. Again, the girl-robots nod. This time, they look at one another and come to a silent agreement about my appearance. Bethany dismisses the girls with a wave. She faces me and says with the sincerity of Chris Harrison at a rose ceremony, "Let's see how your love story unfolds."

Soon after, I receive emails from Bethany and the girls along with pictures of men twenty to thirty years older. The men sit on a motorcycle or lounge on a boat. Bethany and team attach messages exclaiming, *"He's perfect for you!"* or

---

* I'm nothing like Amy Schumer. I thought that line sounded funny. I'm a HUGE fan of Amy. She's a hero to women in so many ways and not just because she's super comfortable with her vagina. She speaks out about things that matter, standing up for all of us in the process. And is this still a footnote or a fan letter? End this thing already!

"We found your love match!" I pass on every single one and say I'm not interested, or flat out lie that I met someone when Bethany persists.

Maybe you're thinking, "What if Bethany found your LOVE MATCH, why so harsh?" And I hear you. I'm the worst. But the whole thing wreaked of an interchange set up long ago. All SHE has to be is attractive (and look acceptable without a jacket). And all HE has to do is pull off the appearance of success through heavy machinery. It's not a hand I want dealt into. This is equal business, friends. Women shouldn't be evaluated like an object sent up for auction and men aren't monetized by their bank accounts. Let's date with self-worth, respect, and find a match who fits our personalities, dietary restrictions, and very particular sleeping habits.

"You can snap a guy, but he has to follow you first and only after he likes four of your pictures, but not group pictures, obviously."—my niece, 17, modern-day code breaker

You're just not that into you

When you've been single since the '70s, you've been on every kind of date. Good dates, bad dates, big dates, little dates. Sporty dates, lazy dates, crazy dates, hazy dates. Dates you loved and some you didn't. Dates who text the next day and those who disappear, leaving you to assume they died in a monkey attack immediately following dinner.

Through most of those dates, I wasn't what you'd call "good at dating." I drank to find self-confidence and ordered another three. Drinking made me sloppy, superficial, and more lost than when I looked for the restaurant at the beginning of the night. I wasn't searching for the right things or behaving in a way to attract a partner who would last. What was worse? I used dating as a barometer for my self-worth. I'd pull up a chair, ready to take a full-scale evaluation from a COMPLETE STRANGER. "Do you like me? Will you ask me out again? Is my nose too big or too small for my face?"

I'd been my ride-or-dye-my-hair for thirty years, yet here I was, handing over my self-worth in one swipe to a person whose name I hardly knew. No, ma'am. No more. No siree "Bob." Is that your name? I didn't catch it.

It took me years to cut-the-shit and get serious about having a real connection. When I was ready, I made a new list of Hot Starters and went further, crafting a complete outline of meaningful traits for a Projected Partner who would last a lifetime. You wouldn't catch me obsessing over my worth and questioning why guys pulled away right when the gettin-got-great. I'd been flaunting this self-love for a while, and I was ready to do some adult-person dating with a clear head and a precise vision for what I wanted out of a relationship.

Self-worth, slam dunk

Letting self-worth take the lead is a paradigm shift reserved for nineties movies with a mother/daughter body swap scenario. It was *Freaky Friday*, friends. Here's what I noticed right away. Lean in, cuz it's a good one ...

For the first time in my life, I'd go on dates, self-worth a-crankin'. Not cocky. Not talking down to waiters and speaking about myself in the third person. But I wasn't desperately sitting across the table hoping my date saw my value. I knew it was there. I knew I was worth dating. And I hoped the person who showed up had a compatible personality, chemistry, and Netflix queue. It wasn't more complicated than that. But, that slight adjustment from, "Do you like me?," to "I'm curious if we like each other?" threw guys off-balance like a trash-talking from Michael Jordan before game seven of the NBA finals.[*] Blank stares. Total confusion. Rim balls.[**]

I'm not saying every guy fell in love with me, of course not, I'm not everyone's type. But it didn't matter. I was good whether they texted the next day or died in that monkey attack immediately following dinner. I was on a

---

[*] I just watched *The Last Dance*.
[**] That sounded dirtier than I intended.

mission to find someone who filled my list, and I didn't overthink it. The freedom that comes with this realization is major, and the reaction you'll get from the person across the table is mind-blowing.

"There's nothing more terrifying than a person who needs no validation."—overheard in my therapist's office

Woman seeking potential

Here's a mistake I've made more times than I can count with a parade of stand-offish suitors. I'd think, "He'll be an amazing partner ONE DAY. I can see a glimmer of a great guy if I close one eye and he sits in direct sunlight."

We're not here to unearth potential like an enthusiastic kindergarten teacher on the first day of the school year.

If that sweet/committed/thoughtful person isn't shining through with total clarity, it's not our job to bring them into focus. You're overthinking your way to poppin' personal growth, find a partner who's done the same, and give them your undivided kindergarten teacher enthusiasm.

Communication breakdown

As humans, we have a tendency to nickname people we date. We take the most obvious thing about a person and voilà, a nickname is born. You have "Mr. Pickle" (because he liked pickleball), "The Other Oliver" (because there was an Oliver before him), and "The Vomit Comet" (let's not relive this). I'm not saying this is a flattering thing to do. If you tell me you and your friend group are above this ancient mating ritual, I'll gladly concede you're a better person than I am. In fact, I concede already.

If you listen closely—people tell you exactly who they are.

Years ago, I dated a guy we'll call, "Aggro Andy." On one of our first dates, Andy said, "I'm a bit of a hot head." I thought, "that's a figure of speech." Not a common figure of speech. Not like, "sweating buckets," or,

"I'm so hungry I could eat a horse." But surely, it was an exaggeration, right?

Andy was attractive and confident, so I ignored my instincts and led with my type. I soon gathered his "hot head" rivaled Chernobyl for nuclear meltdowns. And things imploded after that.

When you're dating, listen LOUDLY. People say, "I've never had a relationship longer than a month." Or, "All of my exes hate me." Or, "Prison isn't as bad as it seems on HBO." You can lie* to your friends. You can lie on social media. Just don't lie to yourself about who's splitting the appetizer at Ruby Tuesday. If you listen closely—people tell you exactly who they are.

Now accepting applications

I'm not going to cross stitch this on a hand towel or put it in a poem. It's not the most romantic notion, but alas, it's true. Dating should be approached like a job interview.

When you look for a new job, experts advise taking as many interviews as possible to get used to the format, hone in on what you want, and gain confidence. Same goes for dating. Go wide on your search and narrow the field after you've collected some resumes. Have fun, keep it casual, and don't make it so serious. If every date is "the first day of the rest of your life," you'll be disappointed when your soul mate doesn't show up for coffee. Date lots of people, chat it up, and learn new things (people are interesting and weird and make amusing stories to tell your friends). When the day comes that you look over your latte and think, "this is the first day of the rest of my life," you'll be calm, cool, and ready to get the job done.

Schmooze without booze

I once drank too much on a date and burst into tears for no plausible reason I can remember. I'm not even a crier. I get the waterworks going maybe once a year. *Maybe*. It's not that I don't harbor emotions, they just aren't

---

* Seriously, don't lie ... gross.

expressed through my tear ducts. I push them way down to the bowels of my body until they're so overwhelming I can't put on socks—LIKE A NORMAL PERSON.

Oh, right … the date. So there I was, bawling on the futon of a guy I just met. He said, "there, there." Or maybe it was, "get out of here." I couldn't hear him over the sound of my wailing. I spent the next few months trying to prove to him I was a normal person who didn't cry on couches unprovoked. Eventually, I gave up, but I took with me a new spirit around drinking and dating.

Most blogs, best friends, and dating experts tell you to tone it down when it comes to drinking on first dates—absolute and tonicly. I say two drinks or less is optimal for a first meeting and here's why. You wake up the next morning and wonder, "Did I have a great time with HIM*, or did I have a great time with four vodka tonics? Because I've gone out with four vodka tonics *many times,* and they always crack me up. I've never gone out with HIM, so it could go either way."

Here's the other part of that equation. *Is this an equation? It seems unlikely.* While drinking four vodka tonics, I'm the *maximum fun times* version of myself. There's no more amusing version hiding in the closet, wearing a tube top, and drinking mimosas at breakfast. Four-vodka-tonics-me isn't really me. It's my pinch-hit personality who comes out now and then to disorient first dates before crying on a futon.

For the first few outings, choose activities such as coffee or walking your dogs. Were it not frowned upon, I'd invite potential partners over for mundane housework. If re-grouting my shower is a laugh riot, imagine our future together? When you first meet someone, make it a dry run. Let them see the real you and get a clear-headed picture of the person who showed up to your date.

Final rose

---

* Or her or them.

Dating should be fun, it should be easy, it should be a scavenger hunt adventure to find a partner with the most items on your list. It shouldn't be something you weaponize against yourself if a date doesn't call the next day. Don't let another person be the high and holy appraiser of your self-worth. Enjoy dating, be clear with your actions and intentions, and "Let's see how your love story unfolds."

Let's overthink it
A guide to dating (a cheat sheet)

- Self-worth is your set point. Whether it means overthinking the exercises in this book or going further with workshops and reading, expand your self-worth, and use it as your permanent guide.
- Two drink minimum. Leave the booze for later. Or, at least know where you stand with alcohol as you enter situations with new people. Make a pact to stay within a limit that works for you on first dates and in situations where trust and safety hasn't been established.
- Date a lot. In the beginning, the more the merrier. Use dating to find your type and your Hot Starters. Have fun and don't take it too seriously.
- Grab the flag. Listen to your instincts and look for red flags as you date. Don't create excuses for people who don't deserve your kindness and attention.
- You first. Before approaching a new relationship, put your personal growth first. Do the work on yourself to provide a solid foundation for a healthy partnership.
- Finally, enjoy dating and don't take it personally.

Brief Thoughts

Actual things I said on a date that didn't turn out great

"You smell like my dad."

"I slept with a blankie until I was in college.
My therapist says it's fine."

"I'm pretty sure I'm allergic to sunshine."

"I think I'm psychic. Not in a cool way, just in a way that's
kind of annoying. You know what I mean?"

"I love my ex-boyfriend, I talk to him all the time."

"I'm not great at drinking. Or driving.
I'm not great at either."

"I used to think I invented the phrase 'Boom, chicka, boom,
boom.' You can't imagine the disappointment."

"Would you mind leaving? I want to spoon my dog."

15 CHAPTER
OVERTHINKING LOVE
that's gonna leave a mark

In my attempt to become a "perfect girlfriend," I almost lost my sanity and my original eyebrows.

I'm twenty-eight living in my hometown of Kansas City, and I'd recently taken a job at a boutique ad agency downtown. The kind where everyone sits around a fireplace and drinks coffee in the morning and plays skee-ball in the afternoon. When they write TV shows about our industry, I cringe at the over-the-top stereotypes, but we were straight out of central casting. It's familial and frenzied and to this day, my most cherished work experience. But this isn't about work ... this is about HIM.

Around the office, there's a hormonal buzz about a certain client who comes in now and then to talk about his brand needs. I'm skeptical about all the hot fuss. What mere marketing mortal is worth this level of Harry-Styles-Hysteria?

Eventually, I lay eyes on the prize, and he isn't just good looking, he's "guy from an underwear commercial attractive." Now, here's the thing. You don't want to go out with a guy from an underwear commercial. Or, lie next to him in your tattered unmentionables. And you never expect that guy to walk into a conference room, sit down, extend his hand, and say, "Hi, I'm Alex." But here he is, and all I can think is "boxers or briefs?"

After our first meeting, I categorize all the reasons Alex must be a terrible, horrible, no-good, very bad dude. A- The tighter the T-shirt, the looser the morals. B- Too much smiling is a sign of mental illness. C- I'd never date a guy whose hair is cuter than mine. In sum, I desperately want Alex to be an asshole, so I can write him off as a cliché, and go get frozen yogurt.

As we continue to work together, I notice Alex is sweet, charming, and unaware of the boyband forcefield that gravitates around him. He's like a superhero who doesn't know he can run through walls. That was Alex, and I was the wall.

At some point, it becomes clear that Alex pays extra attention to me in meetings. He lingers to ask questions outside of my expertise. And for no visible reason I can produce, he *likes* me. Is he looking for free marketing advice? Maybe a gal pal situation? Does he need an organ and discovered we share a blood type?

Under no circumstances will I give Alex a kidney. I've always thought I might do a cool art project with my spare organs later in life, and I'm not ruining a collage for some gorgeous stranger.

One day, Alex asks me to dinner. Still unsure if this is an elaborate kidney harvesting/romance scam, I accept and fall in love with him before the hummus arrives.

Soon, Alex and I begin dating. I'm elated, confused, and nervous nearly all of the time. I feel like a farm girl who won *American Idol,* and I don't know how to act in the bright lights and impractical shoes.

At a loss for how to proceed, I attempt to morph myself into the perfect girlfriend I believe Alex deserves. What do they wear, how do they walk, do they "LOL," or are they more of a "haha" kind of species? I need to know it all, so I can change every last thing about me.

I begin a beauty regimen that borders on psychosis. If there was a section for it in the *DSM5,* professionals would've taken one look at me and assessed, "Oh, classic case of 'dating someone out of her league,'" and they would've prescribed me some Prozac and Botox, and sent me on my way. (Note: I don't attest anyone is "in or out" of someone's "league," but I was less than enlightened at the time.)

Without professional interventions, I'm left to my own devices, applying collagen masks, lemon detoxing, and powering my Pilates. One day before a dinner date with Alex, I visit a local salon to get my eyebrows waxed—as is customary of the perfect girlfriend species.

The technician, Sara, looks at me and says, "Are we preparing for something special?" as she slathers hot wax onto my brow area.

"Yes, I have a date," (with a perfect person) I finish the sentence in my head.

Sara places one cloth strip above my brow and one below on either eye.

"Oh, we'll make you look real pretty," she says.

And RIPPPPP.

"Oh, no," Sara says.

"Holy shit," I cry.

Now, I haven't had my eyebrows done many times before, but it seems "Oh, no" is not an optimal phrase from a person holding hot wax over your face.

Sara hands me a mirror and in place of the four cloth strips are four bloody stripes.

"Oh my god," I panic.

"Your skin ... It's like papier-mache," Sara protests.

"I have a date with a perfect person tonight!" I cry.

Sara suggests using Neosporin twice a day until it heals. I thank Sara for her service and promise not to sue the salon for damages.

I arrive home and look at my swollen, red, bubbly skin in the mirror. At worst, I look as if I've been mauled by a raccoon. At best ... there is no best—it's "raccoon attack" all the way. I shower and hope the miracle of hot water washes away the last hour of my life. One wipe of my steam-covered mirror reveals my prayers haven't been answered, they've been mocked. The four stripes above and below my eyebrows have scabbed, and it appears I'm attempting some form of experimental tribal makeup—and I failed the YouTube tutorial.

I search my closet for the appropriate sweater to pair with a first aid emergency. Cardigan? Blah. Stripes? Hardest of nos. Standard black turtleneck? Yes, the prophylactic of every wardrobe, there to protect you in situations such as this. Alex calls, and I tell him what happened to soften the brow blow. I finish getting ready and walk to the car.

As I'm almost to the door, it hits me—I just propped my head on a little wool pedestal like a bust in a museum. It's too late. I slide into the passenger seat beside Alex, and stare forward without greeting him directly. Alex grabs my chin and turns it toward him, studying my face. After a moment too long, he kisses me and laughs, "I found a restaurant with low lighting. It doesn't matter though, you look beautiful no matter what."

See, you were hoping he said something awful, and we could hate him, right? Not so fast. Act one is always first kisses and second-degree burns. Things don't fall apart until the end of act two.

The end of act two

Overall, Alex is a good boyfriend by my "boyfriend rating scale" I created in eighth grade based on how much a guy resembles the characters on *Saved by the Bell*. He is fun, supportive, interesting, and has a HUGE cell phone.* But strange late-night phone calls, work meetings that don't add up, and trips to the gym when his sneakers are still in the closet, leave me sick to my stomach and questioning my mental reasoning. I don't trust him not to pocket the waitress's phone number when I go to the bathroom. This

---

* Hello, Zach Morris?

makes for some unpleasant brunches of one too many ice teas and one too flirty a waitress. *"No, really I'll hold it."*

Alex says I'm being insecure, and I act insecure, and the relationship continues in a maddening, self-fulfilling cycle. I drive myself crazy pondering, "Just because someone looks like Alex doesn't mean they can't be faithful?" or "Just because Alex has a lot of options doesn't mean he cheats more than the average guy, right?" And I still feel those statements are true. Unfortunately, they were true for Alex.

Off-key

I search for clues of infidelity in everything he does, and every song he sings. Alex is a musician,* and at one point, he calls me into his studio. This is typical, and I enjoy hearing his music. It's part of what works with us, the give and take of collaboration, and a shared love of creativity.

Alex pulls out his guitar, gently strums the chords, and sings the lyrics of a love song. It's soulful, honest—*and one hundred percent not about me.* How do I know? Because I KNOW. Just how you know things about your partner before they even admit it to themselves.

I could write every lyric right here, right now, all these years later and explain how this particular song was about an "old love with chestnut hair" and not about his new partner who stood stupidly in front of him twirling a blonde curl. Alex finishes, and I say, "What's that called?" To which he responds, "She's gone." And soon, I was, too.

At some point, Alex becomes distant and pulls away. I ask what's wrong and he says "he doesn't know what he wants out of life." Which is International Relationship Code (IRC) for "you break up with me, so I don't have to break up with you." I do him the favor, and he has a new girlfriend in less time than it takes me to find a reputable therapist. The woman he's seeing is someone I think he's been talking to for a while. Half of me wants to

---

* Cliché much?

take a victory lap for affirming long-held suspicions that tore at my insides, but the whole of me is too broken for celebration.

I'm not telling you this to make you question your partner every time they leave to work out. This chapter isn't about monogamy. It not about right, wrong, and claiming moral victory. This is still about our all-powerful self-worth. It's still an inside job. I had to learn my attachment style and understand how it kept me cycling in a relationship of insecurity and instability.

It's science!

Somewhere on my self-help sojourn, and way after Alex and I broke up, I came across the concept of attachment theory. John Bowlby, a British psychoanalyst, originated the concept of infant and child attachment theory in the 1950s. Years later, psychologist Mary Ainsworth joined him to create what we understand today as attachment styles.[1]

Until the 1980s, attachment styles were child's play. Then, researchers Hazan and Shaver got involved, extending the thinking to include how adults interact in a romantic setting.[4]

Now, dating and love can't be broken down to facts and figures, but this comes close. When you understand attachment styles, it makes it hard to take things too personally when your dates or partners behave in the predictable patterns that our attachment styles outline for us.

Adult attachment styles are how we relate to other people, mostly in a romantic setting.

Research says our attachment styles develop based on how we interacted with our primary caregivers in our formative years. You don't have to get too clinical or science-y with attachment theory to recognize your style, see it in others, and use it as a guide in relationships and dating. If you want to take it back to the womb, there are many books and resources available on the web to help you do so. A few are listed in the back of this book.

The four major attachment styles

Secure: the VIP, red carpet winner of all attachments

Avoidant: the aloof partner who returns your text four days later

Anxious/preoccupied: the needy/insecure partner

Fearful/avoidant: the "fight starter" who acts out when things get too close

The secure attachment

As is evident by its name, this is the jackpot lottery winner, royal flush attachment style. It's the one to aim for in yourself and the style you should seek in others. It's not to say you can't have a healthy/happy union when other attachments intertwine, but the secure partnership is the best gamble. Secure partners are confident in themselves alone or coupled up. They don't obsess about relationships or whether or not a partner likes them. Their self-worth is solid and intact regardless of relationship wins and losses. They love easily and intimacy is used as a way to get closer to their partner rather than a game or manipulation. Breakups or rejection are seen as part of life rather than an assessment of who they are as a person.

In real life: This is the partner who's up for meeting your family after a few months of dating because they are confident and secure with themselves. They aren't overly anxious about furthering your commitment and if problems arise they know they can handle it with positive communication.

The avoidant attachment

For me, this is the fire engine red flag attachment style. Not because good people can't be avoidant, but because it's a personality that pulls us in and we have no means to change. Avoidant types need their independence and flat out want to be alone (in most cases). They create pockets of closeness with people but disappear at the quiver of commitment. Their emotions are impervious to manipulation because they don't spend much time stressing about partnerships.

In real life: This is the partner who vanishes right as things get good. You have a romantic date, and they pull back to maintain their independence. They may pop up again with a "hey there, stranger" text after they've re-established boundaries, but don't be fooled. They will disappear at the first breach of intimacy.

An alternative to the lone ranger avoidant type is the relationship-hopper avoidant. They move from one partner to another without ever fully investing. They look forward or backward in a relationship, unable to be present with their current partner.

The anxious/preoccupied attachment

This is the unsteady or insecure attachment style. This partner craves closeness and constant togetherness not because of a need for intimacy but because of insecurity within themselves. This partner is overly sensitive and may be suspicious and paranoid even in a loving and faithful relationship. The anxious type may end up in an unhealthy relationship because of their willingness to stay with a partner regardless of bad behavior.

In real life: This partner needs constant affirmation about your feelings and their standing in the relationship. They text repeatedly while you're at work to reassure themselves about your connection despite your consistent behavior and signs of affection.

The fearful/avoidant attachment

Fortunately, this attachment style isn't very common because it's a hard one to have yourself or encounter in the wild world of dating. This partner is avoidant of getting close to others for fear of getting hurt or abandoned. In retaliation, they act out with aggression when they sense closeness from their partner.

In real life: This partner is uncomfortable with intimacy. When closeness occurs, instead of pulling away (see avoidant) they start a fight, possibly name-calling, or worse. It's disorienting and can be very confusing to the other partner.

If reading through the descriptions outlined in this chapter don't help you pinpoint your attachment, there are many quizzes online to help you find your style. Search "Attachment Style Quizzes" and see what you uncover.

What's connecting you?

Where do you see yourself in the attachment styles above? Your style can change throughout your life, and you can possess qualities of different attachment styles at different times (a bit anxious, a bit secure, etc.). Here's the wake-up-call of wisdom about it all ... **You aren't going to give an avoidant partner so much space they finally become secure.** Maybe they decide to change one day, but it won't be because you acted so cool they couldn't resist commitment. Similarly, if someone is insecure, you can love and support them in their effort toward personal growth, but you can't do the work for them. As with everything we overthink, attachment styles are an inside job, too. It's only possible when someone demands a better connection to themselves and decides to change on their own.

In my relationship with Alex, I was acting out an anxious attachment style while Alex was avoidant. At this point in my life I hadn't done the work on my self-worth, so I was insecure and unsure in relationships. Being avoidant, Alex would retreat and then come back. And spin cycle. If I'd been aware of attachments at the time, I would've seen the dynamics in our relationship weren't something I could alter with cute outfits and unscabbed eyebrows.

Act three

Alex and I have spoken over the years to say, "all is forgiven" and "all is well." I realize now that Alex wasn't looking for perfection, and the parts of me he liked—were the messiest. My creativity, my humor, my randomness. I could only see that in hindsight, not in the insecurity of our relationship. If you're curious, Alex is married now. They look perfect together.

Let's overthink it

To get started, grab a notebook, a writing utensil, and open to a blank sheet of paper. Find a quiet spot to sit where you can overthink your thoughts. Let's see how attachments are swaying your relationships right now. List your last three partners or examine your current relationship if you've been with the same person for a long time.

- What attachment styles were your partners acting out and what style were you bringing to the relationship?
- Is there a prominent style appearing in your partners?
- Did you change your attachment style per partner?
- Taking into account what you know about attachments, is there anything you could've done differently with past partners or a current mate to make the relationship healthier?
- Do you find yourself with avoidant partners or anxious partners? If so, do you know why?

If you're married or coupled-up and this chapter leaves you fretting about your partner's less than "secure" style, don't worry. Attachment styles are guideposts for how to interact in relationships. Take your newfound knowledge to your partner or a therapist and discuss better ways to communicate and connect. Also, see the back of this book for further reading on attachment styles.

16 CHAPTER
OVERTHINKING PATTERNS
Is this thing on repeat?

I once found cocaine in a boyfriend's silverware drawer. I know what you're thinking, heavy narcotics should be kept with the drinkware while marijuana is customarily paired with the cutlery.

Despite living alone, the boyfriend assured me it wasn't his. And despite being a full-grown adult who could apply liquid eyeliner, I believed him. That's the thing, relationships are a delusional dish, friends. One day you're on a date with a cute guy, and the next, you're rationalizing there's a cocaine fairy who powders the countryside at night.

When it came to dating, I was often "staring at cocaine in a silverware drawer." My relationships carried an out clause that would eventually present itself. Sometimes loudly—like chopped up powder as I looked for a coffee spoon. Sometimes in a whisper, like choosing a man who's unavailable and can't commit. At some point it occurred to me … my partners weren't the only ones in need of an intervention. I was casting all the wrong things into the Universe and stuck in a pattern that didn't serve my self-worth.

Into my mid-thirties (and after Alex), I'd replaced my anxious attachment style with an armory of avoidant behavior. I went for every guy *who paid little enough attention to get my attention.* I told myself it was normal to go for the chase and enjoy the runaround, but I was dodging vulnerability with the best of them. I chose guys who would mess up, bow out, or even move away. *You're up for a promotion in Tokyo? Take my number.* I threw up my hands and huffed, "Men, right?" But I was in the wrong—willfully waltzing into situations and staying past the point of reason.

Toxic tango

The partners we select are linked to childhood (no surprise there). We choose someone with familiar patterns from our past and pick up the rhythm almost unknowingly. In the simplest example, you grew up watching your parents argue, fight, and endure an unhappy marriage. Twenty years later, you're mirroring the same situation in your own life. **In other words, we find someone doing the dance we already know.** You're lockstep with your past but in the present moment.

We also replay patterns from recent events. For example, in your twenties you experienced a long unhealthy relationship where you were overlooked, treated badly, and disrespected. Maybe it was a marriage or a long-term partnership, but it was a dynamic you aimed to correct on your next go around. Now, you're with a partner who speaks over you, doesn't listen to your needs, and makes you feel insignificant. You sauntered into another relationship with repeating cycles from your past.

For your benefit

It's easy to give a side-eye-to-sky and ask "Why me?" Instead, face yourself and say "What was I getting out of that situation or relationship?" Dating guys who were "unavailable" wasn't bad luck or lousy radar on my part. I was supplying my avoidant attachment style extra style leg room to stretch out and care-not about commitment. **If you're continuing a pattern or a behavior, look for the reward right down to the root.**

For example, let's assume anger is an emotion you'd like to temper. You seem to steam more than the average person and popping off is a regular occurrence. When you delve into your behavior, you see with each outburst, your partner placates and calms you. It's the soothing you solicit rather than the expression of anger.

Use this exercise for any pattern you are trying to understand more deeply. You may uncover an issue you need to examine (such as attachment style) or a reward you could attain in a healthier way.

Road trippin' with the Universe

Remember our hype woman, the Universe? Yes, she's still watching. And she's ready to deliver exactly what it *appears* you want. If during the daylight you crave commitment, but every night you meet your off-and-on, hardly-ever boyfriend, the Universe wonders what GPS you're following.

The Universe is listening to your actions, not your words, and she can't guide you to your destination if you're taking detours with partners (and patterns) who don't serve your ultimate intention.

If you're looking for a stable, committed partner, PROVE IT. Be the person who attracts suitable suitors. Actively search for the qualities you desire in a mate. Be ruthless about what you want and reject people from your life who fall short.

Ask yourself, *"Do I want the Universe to take this person as an example of what I'm looking for in a partner or the kind of people I want in my life?"* If the answer is "no," omit that person from your orbit.

Watch your step

Becoming locked into unhealthy dating patterns is a difficult cycle to spot. There's no intense weight loss or empty bottles piled in your trashcan to taunt your psyche or signal friends as a warning. It may take years to see you're after the wrong things and permitting partners to damage your self-worth or possibly worse. A relationship packed with drama mimics emotions of love, passion, and increased attachment. We become addicted to the rush of conflict and the relief that follows when "I'm sorrys" are said. If you are locked into a pattern that doesn't serve your well-being, ask the tough questions, so you don't return to the same routine again and again.

Let's overthink it

To get started, grab a notebook, a writing utensil, and open to a blank sheet of paper. Find a quiet spot to sit where you can overthink your thoughts. We replay patterns throughout our life unless we stop and do some overthinking.

- Do you see yourself constantly falling for a partner who can't fulfill your needs? Or is there something about your partnerships that ultimately becomes unhealthy?
- When you think about unhealthy relationship(s) that have entered your life, are you type casting traits from your past? EX: Your mother was cold, abusive, or critical, and your relationships reflect this personality.
- Are you mirroring a relationship you saw growing up, or are you replaying a relationship from a past dating experience? Are you "doing a dance you already know?" EX: Your parents had an unhealthy relationship or you had an unhealthy marriage. Now in the present, you continue to date people who repeat this cycle with you.
- Is this coming from your attachment style or their attachment style? Are you looking for love in all the wrong places because you have an avoidant attachment and you hope to never catch feelings? Try to disclose why this pattern replays in your life and design a new one based on intention and action.
  On second thought
  Toxic relationships are a complex and deadly serious subject. That's not what we're overthinking here. I want to

help you understand relationship cycles and patterns you can overthink and reimagine in a healthier way. If you are locked into a toxic relationship, please leave, or get help from friends and professionals. Know that no one should compromise your emotional or physical safety.

17 CHAPTER
OVERTHINKING SEX
missionary accomplished

Half of sex is waiting for it to be over. There's nothing else in life that comes with such build up and anticipation—except pancakes. You work yourself into a lather for this decadent, fluffy breakfast food—the sweet, soft bread drenched in savory mapley syrup and finally, it's here! You have one bite, two bites, three bites "OMG, YES!" And then your blood sugar spikes too fast and you push them away saying, "I finished, get these pancakes off me."

I don't really feel that way about sex. I do, however, feel that way about pancakes. I'm making a juvenile joke rather than opening this chapter with a quip about the first time I had sex (nope) or my most embarrassing sexual experience (nada).

Like a lot of us, I'm not totally comfortable talking about sex. The whole thing is still a mystery to me of sorts. I know you put your right hand here, your left leg there, you shake it all about, and it's over shortly after that. For god sake, I just made a *Hokey Pokey* reference, stop reading this chapter now.

When it comes to sex, overthinking goes into overdrive. It would be easy to turn upside down and go horizontal as we sift through the steamy subject, so let's stay focused on the main lady—the sultry goddess of self-worth.

In the land of dating apps and Bumbled relationships, **sex is a minefield for our self-worth.** We need validation from someone who just saw our Target underwear, and if we don't get it—we'll drain that self-worth tank to the last drop. Or worse? You have sex too soon and try to backfill the relationship part. You've done the deed and now you produce every excuse you can muster, *"I've always wanted to date a person with a pet python."* Wait, what? You spend weeks, if not months, forcing a connection with someone who doesn't deserve your attention.

This is where timeframes and attachment styles come in handy. When we place guardrails around sex, we protect our self-worth and our heart from unnecessary collisions. Timeframes are as personal as sex itself. Sexual appetites, attitudes, and comfort levels differ wildly, and you should act on what feels right for you. Timeframes aren't based on moral judgements, only a structure to help you fill in your feelings within a relationship.

When you look for advice on the subject of "sex and timeframes," there are no hard statistics about the optimal wait time. Relationship experts seem to be all over the bed on the topic, but throw out anywhere from three to eight weeks, sometimes defining it as three dates and eight dates, versus weeks.

"You should wait anywhere from three to eight weeks to have sex with a potential partner."—said no one really

Horizontal-five

For the purposes of this chapter, we'll choose five weeks as our timeframe. Find your number. Is it five months or five hours? Whatever you choose, it's not about gamifying sex. That's not the play here. This is an information-gathering mission, not a grandmaster plan of trickery to gain power or change someone from non-committal to marriage material. The timeframe isn't about making a partner "work for it" or putting up a chase.

Establishing limits is about you. And you owe yourself the
extra effort to decide if this person is worth the lip gloss, to
see their flaws, and fully acknowledge the value they bring
to your life.

**"Oh my god, don't overthink it, or you'll ruin
it."—my friend, way cooler about sex than I am**
Back to attachment

Attachment styles are about intimacy and there's
nothing more personal than the stuff between the sheets.
The tics and triggers of each attachment style come roaring
into the open when sex gets involved. For example, let's
assume there's an anxious partner and an avoidant type. The
couple has sex right away and the anxious partner is inclined
to act needy, clingy, and unsure of the relationship while the
avoidant partner pushes back after too much closeness. You
can see how the relationship is stalled without ever starting
or either partner gets to know the other. What if you have a
secure attachment style and your partner is avoidant? All of
your security about the relationship and ideas about sex
can't change how an avoidant partner will react from the
vulnerability that comes with intimacy.

Using attachment theory, I became a much more
discerning dater. After meeting someone who failed to
communicate, cancelled plans, or felt cold and closed off, I
would think, "He's avoidant," and I chose not to continue
with a personality that would call in their defense the minute
things got cozy. We never made it to the five-week finish
line, so I no longer felt the disappointment of trying to
connect to someone without the potential to reciprocate. If
I slept with them sooner, I would've felt their aloofness and
thought it was ME rather than a fixed attachment style I
couldn't change.

There are endless combinations of attachment styles
we can cook up and compare. Having sex before you see
your date's capacity to connect sets you up for heartbreak
that could be skipped. Put in the time (whether it's five

weeks or other) before the hyped-up hormones of sex get involved.

One and done

Here's the botty line. It's your body. You make decisions about how, when, what, and why. Don't let anyone (especially me) tell you what's acceptable or how to use your sexual expression.

When you're keeping it casual, make sure you're keeping it real with yourself, too. Make choices from a place of fully cranked self-respect, no shame, and no manipulation. If an encounter diminishes your self-worth, or you're hoping it changes the fabric of your relationship from "You up?" to "Coupled up"—overthink your motivations. Sex is good when you love the other person but it's amazing when you LOVE YOURSELF. Protect your self-worth and enjoy your pancakes as often as you like.

Let's overthink it

To get started, grab a notebook, a writing utensil, and open to a blank sheet of paper. Find a quiet spot to sit where you can overthink your thoughts. Write the last three significant relationships or dating encounters. Or, go further back if it turns you on.

- When you look at your last few relationships, at what point did sex enter the bedroom?
- Do you wish it had been earlier or later?
- Did the timing of sex impact your connection or the progression of your relationship?
- Using what you've learned about attachment styles, how did each partner's (your and theirs) play into the encounter?
- Visualization: Picture your self-worth tank from chapter one—full of your fierce, fabulous self-worth. Now think about a sexual relationship you are trying to understand more fully. How did sex

impact your self-worth? In other words, did this encounter fill your tank or drain it of your priceless self-worth?

18 CHAPTER
OVERTHINKING THE ENDING
don't fan the flame

It's Christmas, two thousand-whatever, and I'm dressed to sleigh and ready to be elf-ing jolly about my boyfriend's plans for the holiday. To start, he hands me a card to which he signs, "Have a great year." That's it. No "you mean so much to me." Notta "with love." Nary an "xoxo" in sight. Simply "Have a great year" as if he's my volleyball coach marking up my eighth-grade yearbook.

I don't want to overthink it, so I smile, thank him, and look eagerly as he hands me a gift. I tear at the wrapping to find a candle inside. I like candles. Dare I say, "I love candles." But a candle for Christmas implies something about our year-long courtship. It says, "I was in the checkout line at CVS and remembered you like lavender."

What's worse is the disproportion of my feelings encapsulated in the present in front of me. A present not purchased at a drugstore. A present executed with the coordination of a high school promposal. I hand him his impeccably wrapped gift and say, "Have a great year."

Look, I know what you're thinking, good people can be bad gift givers. But this isn't the case of the rare bad gift giver, yet good person scenario. This is a case of a candle equaling a flame that's about to fizzle. But I took that tiny ember and nurtured it to the point I burned myself and this metaphor to the ground.

Beware of the exit signs

Throughout the years, the biggest mistake I made in relationships is staying too long. Not accepting the ending. Seeing the exit signs and sticking around hoping for a different outcome. It comes back to our first, Beyoncé-level chapter—self-worth. When you do an evaluation of a situation or a relationship and it isn't filling you up anymore, in fact, it's pulling from your self-worth, you're outta there, gone, leaving the bar without a "good-bye" kinda exit.

When things got bad in my relationships, I dug my heels in EVEN MORE. Logic police? I wanted to rewrite the ending and, if possible, the character I was in the relationship. A partner made me feel low, less-than, leveled my self-worth with their thoughtless behavior. So, I stuck the landing, hoping they'd help me mend my bruised self-worth before I hobbled away on one foot. Yikes! **The best predictor of future behavior is past shenanigans.** So, what do you think happened in all of those situations? Patterns repeated and the ending I aimed to edit was now an even sadder tale than where I began.

The big fat-faced fib I told myself was that this shred of a relationship was better than the reward of loving myself enough to shut out people and situations that didn't add up to my full self-worth. Accepting less than you deserve isn't selfless. You aren't needy for demanding what you desire from a relationship. **Be adamant about what you expect from a partner and the Universe. If something is off in a relationship—say it and ask for change.** If it's over or unhealthy, accept your ending, and walk away ready to write your new story.

Missing YOU

At the end, we often miss the person we were during the relationship. You yearn for a part of yourself you believe is lost along with your partner. We see ourselves in others, and an ex may have made you feel "young, artistic, or sophisticated." Maybe you were with someone during a vibrant time of your life and your relationship memories catch some of that color and get painted with the same brush. Of course, we can miss people when they leave— their laugh, the connection, and everyday rituals. *Oh, this is our favorite taco stand!* Just don't spend time missing yourself. You're still here—lessons learned, more resilient, and ready to be an even better partner for the next relationship.

The ex-factor

For years, being friends with my exes was part of my personal brand—like I'm Gwyneth on vacation with Coldplay in the Maldives. I was hung up on it. Eventually, I understood that keeping an ex close to home occupies valuable waterfront real estate in your brain, or your heart, or wherever you want to land it.

I wrestled this one for a long time, so let's get visually nutty to make sure we pin it to the mat.

Imagine you literally have a "relationship ventricle" in your heart. Flowing through your ventricle is the energy of three exs and a person you met at the gym last week. You talk, text, and cuddle if it's raining outside. The Universe glances down, does a quick assessment of your ventricle, and says, "Oh, bummer, they're all backed up in the relationship department." The Universe was about to move a proper partner into your path by way of a meet-cute-coffee-spilling-subway scenario, but now ... that's not happening.

Show the Universe you're open for partnership and not clogged with the energy of old exes and casual hangouts. Free your heart for a new relationship, which may mean being alone as you get the blood flowing again. Remember what we said in chapter sixteen? The Universe looks at who we keep close as an example of what we desire in a partner. **Signal to yourself and the Universe you have space in your life that's currently occupied by texts from your ex.**

As with all rules, there are exceptions, exemptions, and Chris Martins. If you're in a co-parenting situation, I get it. Or, maybe you found friendship in a significant other who just turned out to be "other." Fair. Enough. Be honest with yourself about your intentions and ensure it's a healthy connection for both of you.

Don't be a drama mamma

When you're down-and-out, it's easy to get caught up in your drama. To lie face down on your bathroom floor and woe-is-me 'til morning. We tell ourselves a story about pain and sorrow with us in a starring role. Why? Because tapping into drama spikes those joy-jacked chemicals in our brain, lighting us up, and giving a much-needed bump. So, entertaining our theatrical side is rewarding especially when we're so low there is nowhere to go. It may sound harmless, but it's not. *Don't fall for the drama, mamma.* When we give in to this narrative, we become a victim and subconsciously chant, "I am sad. I am weak," and it sticks. Feel your emotions, live with them for a while, but don't let the darkness hang out like a college kid stealing wi-fi at Starbucks.

I've written a lot about dating the wrong one, but I've dated the right ones, too. Unfortunately, it was before I was anyone at all to myself. I broke up with nice guys, delightful dudes, and supportive men because I needed to figure out who I was solo. It taught me a bit about "timing is everything." But, I also learned that torturing yourself when a date or partner doesn't return your affection is a misguided missile of self-inflicted pain. If we need fixing, we'll look to the relationship for the solution, when it's us who has to do the work.

The reasons people call it quits range from unresolved childhood traumas to not liking how you chew your steak. It's not about us, yet we internalize the attack and use it as a way to injure our self-worth and reaffirm core beliefs from the past (I'm unlovable). When a relationship ends, look for your lesson, and leave it there.

Most of all, don't let the drama of the ending become your new story.

Let's overthink it

I once read an article that said to get over heartbreak you should "burn pictures of your ex." This was back when relationships were marked by a shoebox of images in your closet, not an album on your iPhone. Desperate and dramatic, I grabbed two pictures, sat on the sink in my bathroom, and lit a match to my ex-boyfriend's face. This didn't set off feelings of healing as promised, it set off the smoke alarm in my apartment. I was left with the pain from before and a brown ring of ash around my sink.

People tell you to "get back out there" or "sage your entire house" or "take a hip hop dance class," but there are no flaming shortcuts to the ending. Overthink a few things below, take it easy for a while, and don't scorch yourself in the process of healing.

To get started, grab a notebook, a writing utensil, and open to a blank sheet of paper. Find a quiet spot to sit where you can overthink your thoughts. Use the steps below to overthink the ending of a relationship you are working through.

Check yourself before you reject yourself

- Look at your lessons from the relationship. List them now on your piece of paper.
- Give gratitude for your lessons, whether good or bad. Do this through writing, meditation, or bringing them to mind.
- Clear your conscience. Apologize to your ex if you feel it's needed.
- Cut off communication. This means social media, text, and physically.
- Amp your self-worth through meditation, affirmations, and surrounding yourself with people and friends who know your value.

- Live with your emotions about the breakup and let them go. Don't sink into the spectacle of the ending. Tell your friends and YOURSELF you're done talking about it. Process it and proceed.
- If friendship is in your future, get real with yourself about your intentions before reaching out to your ex and accepting them back into your life.

Releasing relationships or unhealthy patterns (a meditation)

Below is a meditation for releasing old patterns, whether it's a relationship, problematic behavior, or a failure. Use it for any situation you want to *pick up, put down,* and leave in the past. Try it. Then, try it again. And the next day. You'll be surprised what you can put behind you when you actively decide to detach from it.

Find a quiet meditation space. Sit or lie down, eyes closed. Let yourself ease into the moment for a few minutes. Picture a space of calm, peace, and warmth. See your self-worth tank burning bright in the center of your belly. It's hot, bubbly, and glowing with self-love. Give it a color that has meaning to you (gold, blue, red, orange, purple). Your self-worth projects out into the Universe and the image in your mind is warm, colorful, and radiant. Stay here for a few moments as your body fills with the light and heat generated by your self-worth.

Next, bring forward what you'd like to work through or release. Let's say it's a relationship. Picture the person or something that represents that person. (For instance, an object the person gave you during the relationship.) In front of you is a vault-like door, thick and almost impossible to open. On the door is a large wheel, heavy and rusted over from time.

You walk to the door and turn the wheel. It takes effort to move, but eventually, it clicks into place, and you open the door. The person you are releasing walks away from you and through the door. You shut it behind them with a loud THUD. Again, you painstakingly turn the wheel and it locks into place and latches shut. You walk back to your space of light and warmth and sit down. The relationship is locked in the past. Gone from your present. Shut off from your overthinking.

Now focus on your self-worth tank, and see it rise with newly unburdened self-worth. Stay here in this place of peace and warmth for as long as you find pleasing, sinking into the new feeling of lightness and ease. Come out of your meditation and back into your day when ready.

PART IV
THINKING
THROUGH
THE
VOO DOO
THAT YOU DO
(AKA YOUR PERSONAL POWER)

19 CHAPTER
OVERTHINKING YOUR PURPOSE
What do you mean?

In second grade, everyone in my class writes a book for some sort of statewide*writing competition. My handmade book is about a new kid who moves to a new school, and no one wants to be his friend. He has a few tough days (I recall a basketball hitting him in the face), but ultimately, he recovers, makes friends, and creates an app he sells to Microsoft for two billion dollars. Okay, I added that last part. They don't teach climactic endings until third grade.

This little book wins something called "The young author's award" or that's how I remember it. It may have been called "Best book put together with markers and tape award," but let's go with my name. The prize for this award is as follows: A photographer takes my picture posing smartly at a typewriter while wearing a Hawaiian shirt (MOM!). The previously mentioned picture is displayed in the hallway for all to admire. And one afternoon, my parents and I, dressed in our Applebee's best, go see a real-life children's book author speak about her experience as a writer.

From this day forward, I am a writer and no one can convince me otherwise—I have the picture of me in the Hawaiian shirt to prove it. It's not because my book is so

---

* I don't know if it was "statewide." Maybe it was "schoolwide." Or maybe it was between me and one other kid who couldn't spell their name. Memories are a wild animal.

well-written or the words about "the new kid" spout from me like a recently punctured pouch of Capri Sun. It's that the world has given me a purpose, and I enjoy working it through my fingers and rolling it over on my tongue.

Writing has a way of indexing major worries and minor concerns to the dusty catalogs of my mind. When the caffeine is working, and I am too, I feel most like myself. Time freezes, hops, and loses meaning. The only reality lives on my laptop. I look up hours later to see the city had a day, and I had the premise for a short story. Writing is something I own outright, no payments accepted, or license from others required. It won't evaporate like a person I have come to love or admonish me for missteps. I've reached out to it many times over the years, gripping tightly to a purpose I know is meant for me.

If you aren't striking a match about to fire your purpose out of a cannon, that's okay. Maybe you lost your job, got dumped by a *perfect person*, or struggle with a health condition that absorbs your energy. You're on a path and your lessons are leading somewhere.

Five-second rule

In advertising, we often take clients through a series of advertising-y branding exercises. We ask "If your brand was a public figure, who would it be?" If it's a masculine brand, clients always say, "Steve Jobs" (innovative, smart, creative, game-changer)* and if it's a feminine brand, clients say, "Oprah" (brilliant, altruistic, warm, thought-provoking). Every time, without fail.

An exercise I find effective is the "Five-Second Rule." "If you had five seconds to tell people about your brand, what would you say?" It helps drill down to what's

---

* These four characteristics are why people choose Steve Jobs and Oprah to represent their brands in this exercise. However, Steve Jobs wasn't only these shiny attributes. He was also rumored to be cold, mean, and punishing. Oprah has made a profound impact on our culture without so much as a stumble. So, here's the overthink. If a woman was a dichotomy of light and dark in the same way as Steve Jobs, could people see beyond that and choose her to represent their brand in such an exercise? I'm not saying Steve should be discounted because he wasn't lovely at a dinner party— absolutely not. I'm saying, if the same things were said about a woman, how would we react?

meaningful about your company, product, or service. We can't blather on about this and that and how we're all exactly like Oprah. Let's take this exercise out of the ad world and into your life.

> *"If you had five seconds to tell people who you are and what you're about, what would you say?"*

Five-Second Statement
My answer would look like this:
I'm a writer who loves yoga, all things wellness, and my dog, Mo.

It's not showy, it's not clever, but it sums me up in a succinct manner. From that brief sentence, we might pull action steps for my future that look like this: "Maybe you should write a book on wellness." Or, "Why not teach yoga and write for fun." Or, "What if you wrote a screenplay where your dog is the star and falls in love with a pug named Maisy?" All valid suggestions.

Purpose doesn't need to be Grand Canyon grandiose. Your purpose may be: "I want to be a parent. I want to create a loving and safe family I didn't have growing up. I want provide for my parents as the age. I want a job where I work outdoors." Identifying your purpose isn't about seeing your name in lights, it's about finding what lights you up and giving it controlling interest in your life.

Get loud about it
Once you find your purpose, declare it to yourself and others. When we say things aloud they become real to the Universe and our manifestations begin to appear. Tell your friends, your family, and your Uber driver. There was a time I kept my goals to myself because I thought, like wishes, they wouldn't come true if I spoke them out loud. Plus, imagine the embarrassment if I told people I was working on a screenplay and later they asked, "How'd that go for ya, Scorsese?" Then, I started yelling it to the rafters to anyone who would listen. If something falls through and

you have to admit, "I didn't quite get there this time." Good for you for trying. Do you know how many people never even take the swing? Grab the freaking bat, friends.

Universal magnetics aside, expressing your goals makes them more likely to happen from a purely logical standpoint. Here's the scenario. You tell a friend you're studying for your real estate license and they say, "My aunt just opened her own brokerage. I'll give her your name." Coincidental connections can't happen if you keep your purpose tucked tightly under a pillow for only you to dream about.

Believe your own bullshit

TED may not ask me to speak at his Talks about this topic, but I know it has merit. While you're priming your purpose, don't let common sense stand in your way. Push forward with passion and let specifics stand to the side. You want to be an opera singer with a subpar falsetto, you're headed to Lincoln Center. You decide to go to medical school when most of your friends are settled into a steady career, hello doctor. You want to write a hip hop musical about one of our little known founding fathers starring a diverse cast when that's *just not* what Broadway audiences pay to see. You get my point … Revolutionary ideas rarely start with a safe and snuggly premise. Believe your own bullshit and one day, everyone else will see your truth.

Can I have your attention?

When we chat about purpose, it's time to pay attention to our distractions. Distractions steal focus from our goals and let us hide, play small, and duck behind this shrub over here, not living out our purpose. **We produce distractions in our life, so we don't have to face the vulnerability of going for what we want and the risk that comes with not getting it.** What if parenthood is a letdown after years of hoping for a family? What if we try for the big job and can't manage the workload? What if we finally invest in a relationship and the other person cashes out? These paralyzing "what ifs" plague our path so we distract, distract, distract. We take a job that's easy, safe from failure, and not in line with our purpose. Or, we date all the wrong people, so we never have to lose someone we care about.

Distractions often overlap our problematic behavior. For instance, distractions can be drinking, drugs, or gambling. But they're also less sinister and thrive in the get up and grind of nine-to-five. We pack our schedule, never say "no," and cramp our style to the point there's no room for overthinking the bigger questions. In short, we create chaos to pull us from our purpose. Maybe you're always in the middle of a work crisis, or a fight with a friend, or "the worst breakup ever." Chaos takes us on tangents and sweeps us away from reality. If we churn up enough of the frantic stuff, we don't have time for solid questions such as "What do I truly want?" "Am I making strides to get there?" and, "Are these things/people/behaviors/adding to and helping me reach my purpose?"

Good job. Better distraction.

Years ago, I find myself in a full-on distraction with a fairly solid job. I'm unfulfilled, uninspired, and every day I feel my purpose gasping for air. But, I'm busy at work. Things are CHAOTIC. And, it's laughable to think I have time to consider nonsense such as "purpose" and "dreams" as I fight to hit timelines and labor through meetings. Or, that's what I tell myself.

I fume about office politics, who's annoying who, and what's unfair and why. I keep myself in a state of distracted chaos, so I don't have to face a purpose that requires leaving the comfort of my cube. Complaining is easy. Gossip is fun. Retiring this job and aiming for something bigger is ON ME, and I choose distraction over action for years on end.

Eventually, the cost of living this way became too expensive, and I left. This distraction wasn't easy to observe. Life is "chaotic." And, "I'm busy" is a popular chorus in our culture. You have to call it quits with your distractions and let life get quiet enough to hear your purpose shouting for attention.

I've distracted myself with everything we discuss in this chapter. I still do as I listen to a podcast while I scroll through Instagram hopping on one foot. The work we do in this book helps cut down on the chaos. Absolute self-worth means living in the moment with the one-and-only-you. No escape route needed. No distractions in sight.

Let's overthink it

To get started, grab a notebook, a writing utensil, and open to a blank sheet of paper. Find a quiet spot to sit where you can overthink your thoughts. Now, it's your turn to outline a Five-Second Statement.

"If you had five seconds to tell people who you are and what you're about, what would you say?

Breaking it down:

What is the passion that propels you?: *I am a writer*
What is your goal: *To write a book.*
Why are you different: *Make subject matter approachable, easy, and fun.*
Who is your audience: *People focused on wellness and entertainment.*

Now, look at your answers and form it into a sentence or pull insights from the phrases you created. Show it to a friend and see if they have any thought starters. What actions can you take toward your purpose after seeing this new statement?

Gain traction with your distraction

Your distractions may look like many things we discussed in this chapter. Create your own list, pulling from the examples below while considering what keeps you from your purpose.

Ask yourself, *"What's distracting me from my purpose and holding me back in life?"*

Here are a few common distractions you may want to add to your list:

- Going out/partying
- Social media
- Taking jobs that don't fill your purpose
- Sex
- Staying with the wrong partner too long
- TV
- Drama, getting involved in it or creating it
- Helping other people instead of tending to yourself
- Procrastinating
- Substance abuse (pills, alcohol, etc.)

Now that you have your list of distractions, how can you replace some of the time you spend on these activities working toward your purpose? Let's take social media for example. Maybe you decide to limit social media to after eight o'clock every day and commit to working on a business plan for your architectural landscape company for two hours each morning.

You don't have to wake up tomorrow and throw your smartphone out the window. Find a balance. Chip away at your distractions until you've replaced them with healthy habits that edge toward the life you want.

20 CHAPTER
OVERTHINKING REALITY
float your boat

Somewhere around 1983, give or take a year, several families including my own, take a canoe trip to Southeast Missouri. The kind where everyone wears puffy orange life vests and glides down a river, eating soggy sandwiches from a cooler. I'm about six* years old, and my one and only memory (besides the soggy sandwiches) is that my family's canoe flips while going down the river. Whoosh, dunk, cold water rushing by, coolers bobbing up and down, people fishing us out with oars like Kate Winslet on the Titanic, the whole scene.

My sister, age eight at the time, has a similar memory except in her version, she and I endure this early childhood trauma with another family and my poor parents watch from another canoe.

My sister and I only discussed this recently when we brought our competing memories to our mother. As we tag team our way through the family history, my mother holds up a hand as it reaches a tipping point, "I can't hear anymore" she says.

"But, wait, I'm right, right?" I say.

"You're not right, I'm right," says my sister.

It turns out, we were both wrong.

---

* Why am I six years old in all of my stories? Even I don't believe myself anymore.

My sister and I enjoyed a safe trip down the river with my loving parents and *watched* another family flip their canoe—whoosh, dunk, cold water rushing by, coolers bobbing up and down, people fishing them out with oars like Kate Winslet on the Titanic.

We question my mom with the intensity of a prosecutor with nothing to lose. The fact that she was thirty-six at the time of the events was enough evidence against the memory of two girls who recently learned to tie their Keds. She falters a bit on the soggy sandwiches, but I'll allow it.

I wish this whole chapter was about false memories because clearly that. shit. is. nuts, but it's not. I share this to illuminate a major maxim on our self-help canoe trip— we're the hero or the victim of our own story. Whatever you're remembering from childhood is solely your version. **You're creating your reality. Be intentional. Be purposeful. Be the hero. And don't flip your boat for no reason.**

When I learned the concept "your reality is your choice," it kind of freaked me out. Talk about spiritual wackery! You expect me to believe my sister and I are out here piecing together our childhood in opposing fragments like a weird Picasso painting? After a bit of work, I got it. It's an awakening piece of intel to fuel our overthinking. It's about taking control of your mindset, perception, and creating the life you want.

Check your glasses

We all know a person who seemingly has everything but their martyr meter is to the moon. No matter how sunny their side of the street, they complain it's giving them a sunburn. On the other hand, we've met a person who's down-and-out and their only attitude is up. If you're in the midst of struggle, feel it, say it, and lean on friends or professionals. But *pick it up and put it down.*

You aren't an innocent bystander to your attitude or the whims of reality. Actively choose your understanding of the events around you and your reactions. Devise the life you want and be aggressive about it. It's your vision. It's your reality. It's your choice how you see it.

"Folks are usually about as happy as they make their minds up to be."— Abraham Lincoln

This may sound bright and trite and hard to tackle. And no argument with you there. Choosing your reality involves practice. It takes hard work. We need to pay attention to detail when it comes to what's driving our emotions. Discard your negative thinking, implement positive patterns of thought, and put down things from the past that don't serve you. Start with your self-worth and the exercises we talked about in chapter one. Work on a meditation practice to help quiet your mind and picture the reality you desire through visualization. **Aristotle said, "We are what we repeatedly do."** In small bits and bites, you'll replace old habits with new patterns and, in time, you won't have to overthink choosing a lighter reality.

Reality check

For 30 years, I didn't like dogs. Wouldn't mess with them. Never snuggled their face or used a weird baby voice to say, "Does the most gorgeous man in the world want a treat?"

Around elementary school, I visit my grandparents with my sister. As we play outside, I hear a twig snap and an angry growl from behind. I turn to see a steal-colored pit bull *(definitely not a pit bull)*. He bears his teeth and flexes every muscle along his back like a spray-tanned gym bro on Venice Beach. Instead of freezing with fear, my tiny legs scramble up a nearby tree. I splay across the flowering dogwood and stare into the creature's blacked-out pupils.

My sister runs inside, presumably to save herself and enjoy a life as an only child. Thwarting her plan, my grandfather catches site of me through the window and barrels through the backdoor followed by my sister. Grandpa stalks toward my tree-side standoff, waves his pipe, and growls at the canine as only a man of his generation could. The pit bull quickly retreats, and I fall to the ground, kissing the grass with the dramatics of a soldier home from war.

I avoid injury that day. But a fear-based script etches in my mind to be pulled out as a pass when anyone asks "why I don't like dogs."

Decades later, my niece and nephew get a teeny, tiny, cotton ball of a mammal named Mo. At first I did my thing, "I don't mess with dogs, had a bad experience as a kid." Until one day, my sister asks if I'll dog sit for five whole days. Wait. What do I do with him? When does he use the restroom? Why is he staring at me all the time?

When my sister and her family return, my childhood belief is shattered into a million puppy-shaped shards. I am completely in love with this little man and question how I held tight to a story that didn't suit my adult self.

Our childhood narratives should be held up against our current reality.

Limiting narratives can be as fluffy as my tale[*] or serious issues that render us immobile. The stories we remember, repeat, and grab onto like a flowering dogwood often don't align with the person we become. Maybe a story took shape that left you lamenting, "I don't do airplanes," or "I'm afraid of heights," or "I'm bad with technology." It's easy to see how these beliefs limit your growth or at the very least inconvenience your current reality. Challenge your childhood narratives to see if your stories hold up or hold you back.

Eventually, Mo became my dog, and now I know why he stares at me all the time. Why he paces this way or that when he wants his Lambie. How he fake coughs when he needs me to look up from my laptop. That he can't tolerate feet with socks and only stands for bare tootsies in his midst. This is the reality—not a story I told for too long about fear, a tree, and a pit bull (that definitely wasn't).

---

[*] I hate myself for that one.

Let's overthink it

To get started, grab a notebook, a writing utensil, and open to a blank sheet of paper. Find a quiet spot to sit where you can overthink your thoughts.

Love it or leave it

As we continue to explore our purpose, this exercise looks at how we like to spend our time. On the left side of your paper, write things you "love" when it comes to career, work, purpose, however you'd like to frame it. My "love" list would look something like this:

Love

Writing

Psychology/sociology

Networking and collaborating one-on-one and in small groups (coffee meetings!)

Reading

Researching

Wellness

Branding

Design

Advertising

Problem-Solving

Strategy

Now, on the right side of your paper, write things you would rather "leave" when it comes to your career. Erase things that don't add to your happiness, or you aren't willing to do at this point in your life. My "leave" list would look something like this:

Leave

Business matters (taxes, cost analysis, anything with an acronym)

Large group brainstorms (nothing gets done, one person does all the work)

Committees (again, nothing gets done, one person does all the work)

Structured work environment (if there's a cube, no thank you)

Overthink your "love" and "leave" list for a few minutes. Right now, is your day full of things from your "leave" list and not overflowing with the good stuff on your "love" list? What steps can you take to change that? Write action steps next to your "leave" items as you see ways to remove them from your list.

For instance, when I did this exercise, it meant quitting my agency job, moving to freelance writing, and starting this book. It happened in phases over a few years, not the day I took out my pen and paper.

Write your list, meditate on it, visualize the things you see on your "Love" list coming into existence, and don't accept a life you'd rather "Leave."

21 CHAPTER
OVERTHINKING COMPARISON
shaking off the mold

My baby pictures range from genuinely adorable to Gene
Wilder in any movie. As you may have pictured, I was born
with thick, unruly, naturally curly hair. By elementary
school, I sported a style aptly described by my sister as
"high school gym teacher." My mother, a non-curl haver,
couldn't manage my mane so she chopped it to my ears,
brushed it into a helmet, feathered it backward, and sprayed
it with Aqua Net. The firm structure could have protected
me from the worst of dodgeball concussions.

As I got older and took control of my tendrils, I
didn't manage much better than my mom. The number of
third-degree curling iron burns inflicted upon myself
through middle school should've triggered a visit from a
government agency. I was unskilled with a hot tool as I
forced my curls into a shape that resembled the trendy bobs
of my friends. I'd straighten, smooth, and coax my curls to
change. And therein lies the pain of my curly-haired
comrades. During a time, when your singular goal is to look
EXACTLY like everyone else, your hair begs to stand out,
curl up, and say, "I'M DIFFERENT."

My hair and I called a truce years ago. I no longer
spend hours building one bicep as I tug it into unnatural
postures. Wild or straightened by the hands of a

professional, I appreciate my locks and whatever they choose to do each morning.

The mane idea

We all feel the pull to appear like our peers. These days, the disparity doesn't live in my hairstyle but in my home life. I'm over forty and single. Zero marriages, no kids, not even an "Oh, get off your knee, you're embarrassing yourself" kind-of-a-situation. I've been overthinking it all because cultural norms dictate to reach a certain age without traditional milestones insinuates a kind of lacking.

Society says happiness looks like marriage, kids, and a curated social media feed with brunch images and workout wins #blessed. It implies being unmarried is a kind of tumbleweed existence, no commitments to partners, no tether to children, duty-free like the airport.

I wasn't always so solo. For years, I took the passenger's seat—a side-by-side scenario where the only fuel was inertia. Growing up, a best friend was an ever-present pleasantry. In college, my world melded with my roommates' in a mesh of late nights and missed classes. I had serious boyfriends in succession with barely a breakdown in between. At thirty, I found myself single and moved to New York. This was an "all-drivers-seat" situation, and I was unsure behind the wheel. I focused on my autonomy, and I may have over-corrected a little.

So here I am, over forty, single, no kids. *And not looking.* And that may be the hardest part. People presume I'm dying to get married. Men think first date protocol is cocktails and conversation, but by date two, I'll ask them to swing by the fertility clinic. People ask … "Why aren't you married?" or "Did you ever want kids?" I'm not offended. I've pelleted others with the same questions. They are preprogrammed, rote into a script we recite without thought, *"How ya doin? How's the weather? Are you still ovulating?"*

Jokes aside, there are two things people assume about an unmarried person without kids. A- you're selfish. B- you don't like children. I like to think the first one isn't truer for me than anyone else. And I know the latter is false. I love kids. There was a period where I wanted them, but relationships didn't work out, years passed, and honestly, I wasn't all that proactive about becoming a mother.

When I hit the apex of time when it was no longer my question to ponder but Mother Nature's verdict, I was relieved. No more wondering. Fewer people asking. One less choice in a procession of endless decisions. Now I say, "It just kind of passed me by"—cue the pity stares. I realize I need to revise my answer because sympathy isn't what I'm after. I'm not sad about my life sans kids, but I feel the need to apologize, justify, and rationalize it for others.

Here's the big secret. I am happy. Do I want a partner? Sometimes. But I don't feel the gravity of it day-to-day. I do, however, feel the crush of comparison. My life doesn't look like this ... or that ... or land on the right side of the fence, white picket or otherwise.

This chapter isn't a declaration about singledom and society, it's about perception. My perception is that people can't imagine I'm happy alone, over forty, single, no kids. I'm not sure even I can imagine it because it lands outside the margins of "happily" and "ever after" we've read for so long.

Pushing against our perceptions

You have your own perceptions, pressures, and comparisons charging at you every day. They influence your emotions and drive your interpretations of other people's actions. Maybe you've chosen to stay home with your kids and the looks you catch from working moms hit hard. Or, maybe you're the only Woman of Color in an all Caucasian office, and you hold the weight of representation in everything you do and say. Or, maybe you're a sixty-five-year-old professional facing peers half your age with assumptions you're too old to contribute.

"It's not what you look at that matters, it's what you see."—Henry David Thoreau
I could run through every scenario that comes to mind and still miss your experience by a mile. I'm not here to sell a free-hand sketch of life. If you want marriage by twenty-eight and a brood of babies by thirty, adorn your life accordingly. **Don't let a pre-filled list of societal standards tell you what role to fill, when to tap out, or how to act in a given situation.** Start a family at forty or a career at sixty-eight. Be an outspoken activist maven or tuck your thoughts tightly in a journal. Get creative and shape the life you want, and don't fit a mold you were sold years ago.

Let's overthink it

When I tell you about my experience being single, it's based on how I see the world. To reiterate what we've talked about so far, it's my reality, I create it, and I hold the key to altering my perception, good or bad. If you have a perception or comparison that floods your thinking, the first question to ask is "What are you saying to yourself?"

To get started, grab a notebook, a writing utensil, and open to a blank sheet of paper. Find a quiet spot to sit where you can overthink your thoughts. At the top of the page, list a perception you're overthinking. Let's go back to the working mom example, maybe your perception sounds like this:

"How can she be a good mother while working fifty hours a week?"

At the center of this perception, are there things you need to release? As usual, our perceptions mirror our feelings. Maybe you uncover that you want to scale back at work and the guilt shows up in this perception. Or, maybe you live with a core belief "women should stay home with the kids." If so, work through those assumptions now.

Next, pump some positivity into your perception. In our example, it would look like this:

- You're teaching your children the value of work and shared responsibilities between partners, financially and domestically.
- You're setting a positive example for your children and giving them a role model to emulate.
- You're imparting self-esteem in your children.
- While you are at work, your children are practicing social skills while being with other children or an alternate caregiver.

The goal of the exercise is to revamp your perception and find the positives *(like the above)* or the grain of truth (*I really want to scale back at work.*), so you can *pick it up, put it down,* and stop overthinking it.

22 CHAPTER
OVERTHINKING ENERGY
more power to you

Chicago, LA, Kansas City, New York, Chicago, Kansas City
Those are all the places I lived post-college—in that order. If that scattershot list of geography feels like it needs a bit of overthinking, I won't argue with you.

On my second tour of Chicago, I hastily grabbed a lease on a furnished one-bedroom in the Wrigleyville neighborhood of the city. It was dark, damp with a pallor of illness and deficiency. If the lighting didn't spook me, the choices in taxidermy finished the job. Squirrels with human-like eyes followed my moves and questioned my life decisions. An elf-sized door off the closet connected to a *Blair Witch* style dungeon that harassed my nightmares and hindered my dressing routine. The smoke alarm went off twice unprovoked, which led to a not unwelcome visit by the Chicago Fire Department. During a routine trip to the mailbox, I returned to find the door locked. Let me be clear, THE DEADBOLT WAS LOCKED. To this day, I can't puzzle those pieces together in my head.

At this point in my life, I wasn't in a place where I talked about "the mechanics of energy," but I knew enough to say, "this place has bad vibes," and I ran like a girl in a horror movie who you hope is going to make it, but she's slow and never does cardio. My next apartment was bright and airy without a taxidermy squirrel in sight. The energy was high, and I was happy there.

A whole new world

Before I came across vibes, energy, and saw the potential of manifestation, there was no bigger eye-roller than me. I'd watch Disney movies and think, "Give me a break, Aladdin, that carpet would never support the bodyweight of two people." What I'm saying is, I'm not a fairytale person who wishes upon a star. I'm rooted in reality and a frequent dealer of doubt. But I got to the point where all the skepticism was only hurting my eye sockets. The worst part is, I'd actively chosen this worldview. I needed a change, and a shift in energy helped me move out of a place I'd simply gotten used to existing.

Tweak your frequency

Raising your vibration is the grand finale, standing ovation, the victory lap juiciness of everything we've talked about in this book. It's scrapping your overthinking like a pile of junk mail and putting the good stuff to work in a way that turns up the energy on your vibrational frequency.

It means taking all the mojo you've learned and making magic in your life:

- Begin a self-love list.
- Fill your self-worth tank.
- Identify your labels, positive and negative.
- Eliminate negative self-talk.
- Craft your inner monologue with purpose.
- Meditate with light and power (or a practice that is comfortable for you).
- Throw in affirmations from your self-love list in chapter one.
- Create a manifestation list with clearly outlined intentions.
- Put actions behind your intentions.
- Visualize the life you want to live. See the goal in front of you. Feel yourself in this future state.

- Give gratitude for what you have now and the life you're creating in the future.
- Nurture your inner child.
- Understand your type.
- Outline your Hot Starters and revise if necessary.
- Make a list of your Projected Partner.
- Recognize your attachment style.
- Create your own rules for dating and sex but make self-worth your set point.
- Accept the ending of a relationship; sticking and staying lowers your self-worth.
- Love your body.
- Face your control issues.
- Tackle imposter syndrome and know your worth.
- Know your strengths and don't apologize for your weaknesses.
- Let go of unhealthy patterns, own your oops, forgive yourself.
- Release your shame.
- Find your purpose.
- Stop distracting yourself.
- Create your reality.
- Lose limiting narratives
- Quit comparing yourself to others.
- Reframe your perspective.
- Amp your energy.
- Pick it up.
- Put it down.
- Leave it in the past where it belongs.

Vibes 101

On the one hand, "vibes" need no introduction, no coming-out party, no MTV-style *Sweet 16*. You know what they are. You use them as an unseen tour guide and randomly drop them into conversation. Everyone has walked out of a tense meeting and said, "Whoa, that room had bad vibes." Or, met a new person and declared, "She has really good energy." But on a broader level, you may not

understand all the hoopla that goes into "raising our vibrations." It goes a little something like this:
1- Our thoughts, emotions, and actions generate a vibrational energy.
2- That energy aligns with the experiences (people and events) that come into our life.
3- Good energy equals good experiences (and a good life).

Am I making bad things happen?

Right now, you may wonder ... if good energy equals good things, bad energy makes my sink clog and my face break out before a date. Fear not the wrath of the Universe. If you happen to be in a low vibration period, think of it as an ebb or a lull. You're not taking control of your life or rolling out the welcome mat for the cosmic goody bag available to you. If you have a bummer of a summer and wallow for a while, the Universe won't assign punishment. When you place energy back on your agenda, the Universe will be ready to meet.

That FOR-letter word

FOR-GIVENESS, it's a tough one. But it's a vital concept when it comes to energy. Living with resentment is an energy vampire worthy of a strange accent and a castle in Transylvania. When someone does us dirty, it's easy to carry ill will. You don't need to ascend to forgiveness the day your business partner makes off with your money. Anger is a valid emotion. Feel it, sit with it, but don't let it move in and drain your energy for the next season of your favorite Netflix show.

When someone acts out or treats you badly, the storm brewing for them is much worse than the clouds you observe on the surface. That's a fancy way to say: choose empathy over anger. Understand they're in pain and use compassion to release you from this matter. Leave the situation in a way that honors your thinking, character, and self-worth. Being a bigger person raises your vibration and excuses you from the toxic ties of this situation.

"There is no revenge so complete as forgiveness."—Josh Billings

If empathy isn't your angle, consider winning. When another person burdens you with bitterness, they lower your energy and interfere with your manifestations. They ruined your relationship and six months later, they're tearing up your vibe game. As long as you cave to anger, you're handing over your power to this person, thing, or problem. *Pick it up and put it down.* Forgive yourself. Forgive them. And cut the energy of this experience at the root, so you're directing your vibrational future. Checkmate. You won.

Circuit training

"Good vibes" isn't just a phrase to print on a poster. As mystical as it is to tap into energy, it takes work. You can't go from boo-hooing on your bathroom floor to sitting on the couch talking to Oprah about "living your best life."

Vibrations aren't a switch. They expand in increments and grow over time. It takes practice, repetition, and commitment to your goals. For me, right away, the world looked brighter, things felt lighter, and after I put in the work, I noticed some of my manifestations appeared in my life. It took patience, but I raised my energy to the level I was envisioning and feeling.

No, really ... explain it to me

Think back to chapter one and two. When you've mastered an inner monologue slam-packed with elevated thoughts and positive labels, you raise your vibration. That high vibration aligns with the intentions and manifestations we listed in chapter five. We have to raise our energy to the level of the experiences, things, and even people we're inviting into our life.

For example, on your manifestation list, you have the intention "Making partner at my law firm by the end of the year." Right now, you're in a bad place, mind-numbing your way through the day. That low energy isn't moving you anywhere because it's not at the same high-vibe level as "partner." You do the work ... (manifestation, meditation, affirmations, visualization, monitoring your inner monologue, stopping negative chatter, creating a lighter reality, and everything else we've discussed) and you raise your energy to the frequency of "partner at your law firm." Now, that experience can greet you, meet you, and usher you into the corner office because you exist at the same energy level.

It's not as simple as putting on a happy face and skipping around the courtroom. **Carl Jung said, "One does not become enlightened by imagining figures of light."** That means we have to clean out the basement of our past to create space for the high-vibe renovation we're imagining. Hopefully, that's what we've been overthinking since chapter one. Boosting our self-worth, looking at our labels, revising our inner monologue, sacking up the garbage of our overthinking minds, and tossing it in the bin.

If the tools in this book don't get you there, please see references in the back, reach out to a therapist, or do whatever voo doo that you do to raise your energy to meet your manifestations and the life you deserve.

Let's overthink it

Let's put some practical application around our understanding of vibrations, recognizing things in our everyday life that affect our energy. To get started, grab a notebook, a writing utensil, and open to a blank sheet of paper. Find a quiet spot to sit where you can overthink your thoughts.

List three things that lower your vibration:

Here are a few examples, but please make a list of your own. Energy is personal to your preferences.

- Unhealthy relationships
- Negative self-talk
- Consuming too much negativity/outrage through news, social media, TV, etc.

List three things that raise your vibration.

Here are a few examples, but please make a list of your own. Energy is personal to your preferences.

- Time with people I love/Chats with friends I love
- Seeing art museums/theater
- Yoga

Below is a meditation to help raise your vibrations. Use it to move out of a low energy period or to help you kick up your frequency before a big event.

Raising your vibration (a meditation)

Find a quiet meditation space. Sit or lie down, eyes closed. Let yourself ease into the moment for a few minutes focusing on your breath and quieting your mind. Think about a space of calm, peace, and warmth. Sometimes, I listen to binaural beats[*] during this meditation to mimic the sound of energy and vibration through my headphones.

Now, visualize your energy like a speedometer. See the line on the speedometer slowly move all the way from the left to the right, feeling more energy and higher vibrations at every point. Continue visualizing yourself in a place of light and warmth. Now, your vibrations are off the dial of the speedometer, all the way to the right, buzzing and vibrating with warmth and energy. This is where the binaural beats become helpful. If you try to visualize your energy along with a high tone frequency, it may be easier to sense the vibrations. Stay in this place for five to ten minutes (or for a full twenty-minute meditation if you'd like).

When you come out of your meditation, things should be brighter and you may notice an actual uptick in your energy. Carry this high vibration with you throughout your day.

---

[*] Google "binaural beats for meditation." You'll find a library of free tones on YouTube. Brown noise is also soothing and may help with your meditation.

23 CHAPTER
OVERTHINKING IN YOUR UNDERWEAR
getting down to the skivvies

A few years back I went to Europe alone—Paris, Rome. Everyone said, "Oh, so this is an *Eat, Pray, Love* kinda thing?" I'm a huge fan of Elizabeth Gilbert, I just didn't have as high of hopes for my trip as her best-selling odyssey. I wanted to see sights I'd only read about, write in cafés that look like postcards, and wear scarves that made me seem interesting.

Friends and family wonder if I'll get lonely or lost. They worry I'll be pickpocketed or worse. Some think it's brave or inspiring, but mostly a bit weird. I don't get lonely. I get lost, but in a lazy way that leads to something new around every corner.

One night in Paris, I sit at an outdoor café eating a dish I pointed to on the menu and am pleased to discover tastes like grilled cheese when it arrives. I sip my drink, look at the passersby, and think to myself like Mary Tyler Moore in a 1960s sitcom, "Wow, this is just about the most fun a gal can have!" Sure, who can complain about twilight in Paris? But it's more than the Eiffel under the stars. I've done something I wanted to do for too long, I've taken myself to Europe.

For years, I said I'd get to Europe "sooner or later." Later with the right partner. Later when I had more money.

Later with my best friends. I was in my thirties and still looking for "later."

In my head, Europe had to take shape on a romantic trip for two or right out of college with a gaggle of friends and a backpack. I defined my dream in absolutes and erected walls that wouldn't let me near it.

In about two weeks' time, I booked a trip, grabbed my passport, and took down my walls along with the labels, negative chatter, self-doubt, past failures, distractions, and excuses that held me back and kept me stateside. As with most things we make precious and lock away for later (the big job, the house, the baby, the relationship, the goal, or just plain self-acceptance), crossing the pond didn't require approval from others, outside forces, or a dinner companion. As it turns out, even my trip to Europe was an inside job.

"A life unexamined is not worth living. But a life of overthinking isn't either."

I hope you've gone through these chapters, learned something, and left it there, ready to go out and live the life you deserve. No more summoning ghosts from the past or deploying negative thoughts to tear us down. Some of these exercises should be tucked away and taken out now and then. My meditation practice grounds me when I need it and bolsters me with what I want. We've discussed better ways to see ourselves, choose partners, and consistently fill our self-worth tank, and those are rituals to rally behind every day.

You don't need me, this book, or even the Universe to sign a permission slip for the life you want. It's your choice to negate the nonsense and gather all the goodness available to you. The career—yes. The partner—hell, yeah. The totally traditional or utterly unconventional family structure—it's yours. A little farmhouse outside of town with a blue door and llamas in the backyard—it seems possible, but we need to check zoning laws in your town.

You have the power to do your thing. Do it now without another minute overthinking in your underwear.

with love and overthinking-
Lindsay

Brief Thoughts

Things we're done overthinking

That last text we sent to our ex ... at two a.m.

How our chin looks in selfies.

Selfies.

That thing that happened in high school.

If our butt is too big or small or flat or round or lumpy in
that one weird spot.

What their mom thinks of you.

If we're too extroverted or introverted or 'verted in any way.

What if we had gone to that school?

Or taken that job?

Or chosen that partner?

Or tried out for the play in fourth grade?

**What if we pulled up our big girl pants and
loved ourselves already?**

AFTERTHOUGHT

This isn't my first book. I've written unfinished or polished and enthusiastically rejected books, screen plays, short stories, and even poetry. There was the greeting card company that wasn't. I won't opine, "defeat is the ultimate guru." No … here's the thing about all of that effort. The craft of writing is my purpose, passion, and I'm grateful it rests at the belly of my self-worth, urging me forward. But, something else was also propelling me. A need for validation. A wish for someone, anyone, to see me and say I was okay, enough, cool as a cucumber.

I conflated a search for purpose with a gnawing for validation. I toiled away en route to my pursuits, but my energy was aimed in the wrong direction. I knew I needed to face my past, alter behaviors, and blow the roof off my self-worth. But I hoped there was a "success-loophole" where I skipped the icky self-reflection and moved straight to wearing "Good Vibes" T-shirts and snapping duck-faced selfies in the mirror.

As you read, I had to do the work, there were no loopholes, and I'm still not a sexy duck no matter how hard I pout. So, all these years, tries, attempts, failures, and an entire book of self-worth later, I discovered the thing I woefully desired.

I want you to love, enjoy, and grow from this book, I really do. But on my way here, I found the validation I needed from all of those endeavors. *Ain't that a kick in the underpants.* It's also the ultimate high-five and Hallelujah of self-help and manifestation. Feel "as if."

You don't need to achieve anything, nothing, notta damn thing to feel "as if" you are worthy. Because self-worth is your real purpose—loving yourself is the whole damn job.

And, another thought

Can you imagine an overthinker writing a book on overthinking? Can you even fathom the thoughts I've thunk while thinking through the thoughts on these pages? Will you like this book? Will you hate this book? Will you find it useful? Will you find it too useful? Will you use it as a little stand for your toilet paper in your bathroom and suddenly a book I've thought all my thinking into is a toilet paper stand book. I actually don't mind, it sounds adorable. Please proceed and send pictures.

I hope this book made you laugh, think, overthink, and sit in your underwear wondering, "Is a self-worth tank the stupidest thing I've ever thought? Or, the smartest?" We may never know (shrugs).

As an unproven author, I say this to you wholeheartedly, thank you for trusting me with your time. I've loved every second overthinking with you. I hope we get to do it again someday.

Below is a list of resources and teachers that illuminated my learning. I hope you check them out.

Have you read?
You're a Badass by Jen Sincero—If you're thinking about manifestation, self-worth, the ego-self, and your own badassery on almost every level.

You're a Badass at Making Money by Jen Sincero—If you're thinking about reforming your attitudes about money, this is the book for you. Beyond the dollars and sense, Jen hands out spiritual brilliance in a hilarious way.

The Year of "Yes" by Shonda Rhimes—Yes, that Shonda Rhimes. *Grey's Anatomy,* Shonda Rhimes. I'm going to call this "required reading for introverts." I nodded along so much reading this book I needed to see a chiropractor afterwards.

EXTRA: Shonda has a Masterclass called, "Writing for Television" on Masterclass.com. If you are interested in this mode of writing, Shonda breaks it down and makes it entertaining.

Why Him? Why Her? by Dr. Helen Fisher—If you're thinking about how your past as well as your personality plays into how we select partners. If you are new to Dr. Fisher, do a quick Google search, listen to her TED talks, and read her articles in *The New York Times*. She's a fascinating thinker in the area of love research and how we interact as human beings.

Spirit Junkie by Gabby Bernstein—If you're thinking about manifestation, meditation, the ego-self, and many other concepts I don't cover in this book, Gabby gets into it in an honest, revealing, and understandable way.

Attached by Amir Levine, M.D. and Rachel Heller, M.A.—If you're thinking about attachments and how they play into your relationships and self-identity. If I whet your whistle on attachment theory, you'll be singing a new tune after you read this book. It's the ultimate guide to adult attachment theory.

The Dark Side of the Light Chasers by Debbie Ford—If you're thinking about projections, the shadow-self, or what we talked about throughout as "labels." Ford is like a drill sergeant demanding accountability for your thoughts, actions, and emotions. It's an illuminating look at your past and a treasure map to finding self-love. If you're looking for self-help boot camp, you'll find it here. If the first section of our overthinking work spoke to you, pick up Debbie's book.

The Shadow Effect by Deepak Chopra, Debbie Ford, and Marianne Williamson—If you're thinking about learning more about the concept of "shadow" from multiple thought leaders with different perspectives.

Becoming Supernatural by Dr. Joe Dispenza—If you're thinking about energy and using your mind to heal your body and create your reality.

Big Magic by Elizabeth Gilbert—If you're thinking about creativity, Elizabeth has a gorgeous way of describing human interaction and the world around her.

Professional Troublemaker: The Fear-Fighter Manual by Luvvie Ajayi Jones—
If you're thinking about using your voice of finding it, Luvvie will
inspire you with her message. "Trouble-making" is being real, speaking
your truth, and so much more. Luvvie has a hilarious way telling stories
and sharing advice in this entertaining and impactful book.

Daringly Greatly by Brene Brown—If you're thinking about vulnerability
and how to be the most authentic version of yourself. Also, watch
Brene's Netflix Special "The Call to Courage."

Love Warrior by Glennon Melton Doyle—If you're thinking about past
relationships, body image, spirituality, and more. Glennon helps you see
yourself through her revealing story in this deeply personal book.

Ask and it is Given by Esther and Jerry Hicks—If you're thinking about
the Law of Attraction, manifestation, and using energy to create the life
you want. This book gets trippy with the Law of Attraction and energy
work, but it's worth the read if you want to explore the subject.

Can't Hurt Me by David Goggins—If you're thinking about unlocking
human potential (his words). Retired US Navy SEAL, David Goggins
gets incredibly vulnerable, telling his life story of survival and creating
himself from nothing while helping you look at your own life with real
strategies and tough love. This book is fantastic as is demonstrated by
YEARS on the best-seller list. I recommend the audio version where
David adds extra, podcast-style commentary and advice.

If you're thinking about a laugh
The Girl With the Lower Back Tattoo by Amy Schumer
Is Everyone Hanging Out Without Me? by Mindy Kaling
Bossy Pants by Tina Fey
Me Talk Pretty One Day by David Sedaris
Dear Girls by Ali Wong
Not That Kind of Girl by Lena Dunham

Have you listened to?
10 Percent Happier with Dan Harris—If you're thinking about meditation.
From talks with meditation teachers and gurus to free guided
meditations, Dan Harris is your ultimate meditation hero. Check out his
book by the same name.

The Goop Podcast—If you're thinking about anything GOOPY from
energy work to body image to vaginal eggs, they cover it here. Don't let
naysayers steer you away, this podcast speaks to experts and celebrity

guests on spiritualty, wellness, and a sphere of self-help and psychology subjects in a deep and honest way.

We Can Do Hard Things with Glennon Doyle, Abby Wambach, and Amanda Doyle—If you're thinking about diving head first into self-love with thinkers of today, this trio will take you there. Their honesty and willingness to expose their truths while helping you look at yourself is inspiring and powerful.

On Purpose with Jay Shetty—If you're thinking about mindfulness, psychology, and self-love. Jay is a life coach and former monk who helps expands your thinking on ideas like mindfulness and purpose. Jay also has a book called, *Think Like a Monk*.

Have you logged on?

tobemagnetic.com led by Lacy Phillips —If you're thinking about committing to a self-help workshop that guides you step-by-step through manifestation, meditation, the shadow self, understanding your inner child, uncovering subconscious blocks, working through relationships, manifesting money, and so much more. Lacy's teaching is easy to follow and most classes include guided meditations and journal prompts at the end.

Coursera.com—If you're thinking about taking online courses on mindfulness, psychology, and even happiness, Coursera allows you to log on for free (in some cases) to University level classes and learn from the comfort of your couch.

If you're thinking about getting help

If you struggle with an eating disorder, please call 800-931-2237 and connect to the National Eating Disorder Help Line. Visit www.nationaleatingdisorders.org to find treatment.

If you need support for substance abuse and mental health, please visit www.findtreatment.gov/ to find resources near you.

If you or someone you know are in an unsafe or abusive relationship, please call the National Domestic Violence Hotline at 800-799-7233. Or, visit www.thehotline.org/ for access to resources and support.

Visit www.findahelpline.com for a library of resources across the United States.

Notes

1. Ainsworth, Mary and John Bowlby, "The Bowlby-Ainsworth Attachment Theory." Published online by *Cambridge University Press*: 04 February 2010, (notes to chapter fifteen, chapter seventeen).

2. Fisher, Dr. Helen, *Why Him? Why Her? Finding Real Love by Understanding Your Personality Type*, (New York: Henry Holt and Company, LLC, 2009), (notes to chapter thirteen).

3. Ford, Debbie, *The Dark Side of the Light Chasers*, (New York: Riverhead Books published by Penguin Group (USA) Inc. 1998), (notes to chapter two and three).

4. Hazan, C., and Shaver, P. R. (1994). Attachment as an organizational framework for research on close relationships. *Psychological Inquiry, 5*(1), 1-22 https://doi.org/10.1207/s15327965pli0501_1 , (notes to chapter nine).

5. Hicks, Esther and Jerry, *Ask and it is Given,* (California: Hay House, Inc 2004), (notes to chapter five and chapter twenty-two).

6. Imes, Suzanne, PhD, and Pauline Clance, PhD, "The Impostor Phenomenon in High Achieving Women: Dynamics and Therapeutic Intervention." *Psychotherapy: Theory, Research & Practice, 15*(3), 241–247. (1978), (notes to chapter nine).

7. Levine, Amir, M.D, and Rachel S.F. Heller M.A., *Attached. The New Science of Adult Attachment and How it Can Help You Find — and Keep — Love,* (New York: Penguin Random House, LLC, 2011), (notes to chapter fifteen, chapter seventeen).

ABOUT THE AUTHOR

Lindsay Bruno spent the last twenty years as a copywriter in the advertising field. She's worked in Chicago, New York, and her hometown of Kansas City on large national brands and small mom-and-pop clients. Along the way, she's written long-form fiction, screenplays, and essays. In 2018 she resigned the full-time grind of agency life to give her creativity room to think—or *overthink* as it turns out. She currently works as a freelance writer to support her dog's lavish lifestyle. This is Lindsay's first published book.

Follow on Instagram @overthinkinginyourunderwear
Please consider reviewing this book on Amazon, it helps other readers find and enjoy *Overthinking In Your Underwear*.
Book cover design by Hello Big Idea @ hellobigidea.com

Made in the USA
Monee, IL
13 April 2023

31330092R00105